HOW TO BE AN ARCHITECT DEVELOPER

AMANDA BAILLIEU AND GUS ZOGOLOVITCH

RIBA Publishing

[redacted]

To Paul and Patti, Z, R, O and F,
thank you for all your help and support

Reprinted 2025

Published by RIBA Publishing, 66 Portland Place, London, W1B 1AD

ISBN 9781914124938

British Library Cataloguing-in-Publication Data
A catalogue record for this book is available from the British Library.

Commissioning Editor: Alex White
Production: Jane Rogers
Designed and typeset by Sara Miranda Icaza
Printed and bound by Pureprint Group Ltd
Cover design: Sara Miranda Icaza

www.ribapublishing.com

FSC www.fsc.org
MIX
Paper | Supporting responsible forestry
FSC® C022913

ACKNOWLEDGEMENTS

Many thanks to everyone we interviewed for this book.

Russell Curtis deserves a special shoutout for his helpful suggestions and for sharing our belief that there should be more enlightened policies around land disposal and home building that would prioritise better design and new ideas over securing the best price. Thank you to all those who read the manuscript and to the RIBA for believing in this book from the start.

The book grew out of an idea we had over a drink in St John in Clerkenwell. We both felt that while architects have some of the skills required to become developers, there is nothing in their training that prepares them for such a different role. At the same time, more and more architects were asking us about becoming the client so we set up Developer Collective with a mission to provide them with a crash course on how to become a developer. We ran courses and conferences on what we felt architects needed to know, from establishing the viability of a project to marketing and selling what has taken years to design, finance and build. The book is a culmination of everything we've taught, discussed and learned over the years.

FOREWORD
by Roger Zogolovitch

The profession of architecture has moved a long way from my Architectural Association student days some 50 years ago. At that time, the professional code of conduct prevented architects from being directors of either development or construction companies. Being an architect developer was also prohibited. Development had no position in the architectural debate.

I remember the moment when my tutor gave me a short development appraisal that she had obtained from one of her developer clients. This, along with the discovery of the *Estates Gazette (EG)*, opened a window onto a world which, up to that time, had been hidden from view. As I probed further it appeared that making projects happen needed engagement with the mercenary world of commerce.

Role models to learn from were thin on the ground. The first to mention is Richard Seifert who, although he remained an architect, built a highly successful practice because of his skills in adding value for his clients. The second is the American John Portman, who established himself as an architect developer through his understanding of the entire development process.

Richard Seifert was attuned to his clients' financial ambition and used his architectural skills to optimise the commercial value from their sites. I started my architectural education in 1966 just as Centre Point finished construction. Every day as I passed through Tottenham Court Road station, this towering structure with its powerful facade of precast concrete panels both caught and demanded my attention. Oliver Marriott published the *Property Boom* in 1967, which gave a clear explanation of the post-war property industry, including an explanation of how Seifert won planning consent for Centre Point. His offer to his clients of simply satisfying their commercial requirements enabled him to be prolific in his output despite being much maligned by his architectural peers. His approach won trust from his clients, who then permitted him his aesthetic freedom. His buildings have stood the test of time and they now form part of our collective idea of London architecture.

John Portman, operating in Atlanta from the 1950s, pioneered the role of architect developer. He stated that he was driven in his quest to realise projects where he could make his contribution in 'a role that can produce more for society'. He told the familiar story of a young architect setting up in practice, waiting for the commissions to roll in and feeling disappointment when his clients' demands didn't quite match up to his architectural ambition. He set himself the task of understanding the wider development process from site acquisition, concept design, feasibility, financing, marketing and delivery, in other words the world of projects beyond architecture. With this understanding he was able to become an architect developer and create his own developments. He started with the Atlanta Merchandising Mart in 1956 and continued to evolve a brand and development typology of hotel and retail buildings, built around his trademark soaring internal atriums. The Hyatt Regency in Atlanta was the foundation of his approach. Having made the move to development he was able to control this process and use his creativity to support his role of architect developer over a long career.

My own choice of changing career was made in the late 1980s after building Royalty Studios as a developer. It consisted of 16 new-build studio/offices, constructed on a gap site off Ladbroke Grove and a short distance from Portobello Road in west London. At the time, it was not an acceptable or even recognisable commercial location, which made it both a challenge and an opportunity.

When this development was being designed I was still a partner at CZWG Architects. I used the project to pursue research for a simple but robust form of construction. I found that precast concrete floors could span 7m and therefore used that dimension to set the width of the individual studios. To create a warehouse look we used white painted bricks as an internal skin. To heat the space we put boilers at the top of the stair core and fed hot water down the front and back walls using a ladder arrangement of radiators. On the front and rear walls we used industrial metal windows. The windows were wide and to support the facade above we modified the Victorian-brick jack arch, enabling us to use three windows to span the distance. Each window was neatly supported by a precast keystone fixed to the floor. As both the architect and the developer I was able to make my own decisions and control every detail and the overall vision of the final building.

I describe this at length because it represents the essence of the architect developer: the need to take full responsibility not only for every last detail but also for the project's financial success. The projects take longer to complete but you are in control, setting the priorities on design, buildability, marketing and funding.

As an architect developer, you need an alternative vision whereby the journey starts not with a client, but rather with a site or building. You also need the additional skills that this book sets out well and realistically. They are skills that I learnt and which improved with every project I undertook. The reward is both personal and financial. The personal reward is realising your dream and vision for a project; witnessing an idea generated by you and driven forward by your own architecture. The financial reward is achieving the added value from your own enterprise.

Roger Zogolovitch, Architect Developer
Founder, Solidspace

CHAPTER 1

WHY BECOME AN ARCHITECT DEVELOPER?

'Making money out of property development' is one of the top Google search terms and there is no shortage of experts giving advice on how best to do it. Some of the advice is useful and, after reading it, you may be left with the impression that anyone can do it. To a certain extent you'd be right; property development is not that complicated, it's just risky. Successful property development is about making the right decisions at the right time and about being able to deal with everything that can go wrong along the way.

Many architects have tried their hand at a small development project – whether their own home or refurbishing properties and selling them on. But fewer have made the leap to become a fully fledged architect developer. This is not down to a lack of determination, but more from a nervousness that they do not possess the business skills required.

Architects also know the pitfalls. They know, for example, that planning can derail projects (and often does) and they know that choosing the right contractor can be the difference between a project running smoothly and mayhem. This makes them more cautious. If they are running a small practice, they are often time poor and development can be very labour intensive, which is a further reason why it can seem like a diversion that can leave you horribly exposed if something goes wrong.

So, can architects ever compete with a seasoned developer? The answer is 'yes', particularly with awkward inner-city sites where architects can spot opportunities and creative solutions that a non-architect developer will often miss.

This is how Maria Sjölander and Marco da Cruz made their mark when they spotted the potential of Birmingham's industrial buildings years before conventional developers arrived on the scene (see chapter 4). They pioneered a much-copied model of inner-city living. They did so aware of the risks but also knowing the market was ripe for high-quality contemporary homes in the city centre.

Almost all of the architects interviewed for this book used their first development as a springboard, not quite knowing where it would lead and unsure of when the next opportunity would come along. Some have chosen to remain small developers while others have decided to work at a bigger scale. In all cases working on their own development has given them an invaluable insight into the property market as well as opening their eyes to the true cost of the decisions they are making on behalf of clients.

But let's start with motivation. Why would you want to borrow millions of pounds and spend four or five years, or even longer, managing a process that could be thrown off course at any point? The developer's answer is profit, otherwise the project cannot proceed. For architects, however, the reasons are slightly different and may relate to the challenges they face generating enough well-paid work to sustain them over a lifetime.

Another factor for architects is that the intangible rewards may be greater. Often for a young architect entering the profession after seven years of study, there can be a sense of frustration when they discover how little input they have in the process and how much their day-to-day work is simply about being a small cog in a larger machine. This frustration is not new and many architects have found an outlet in teaching or research. Yet as valid as both these endeavours are, this could be seen as a retreat rather than engagement with the act of producing architecture. Others are experimenting with an alternative model to conventional practice; one offering more freedom and more control. One of the most celebrated examples is Assemble, whose self-initiated projects offer agency and independence, something much admired by colleagues working in more conventional settings. But as Assemble admits, it is difficult to make this model work on larger projects when the business has to sustain 20 people or more.

Yet linking the experience of Assemble and that of the architect developer is a trend towards expanding the architect's skill set into new forms of practice where they can engage with all aspects of making buildings and take back control of a process that many feel is being eroded.

For Craftworks' founder John Smart (see chapter 4), this question about how practices currently operate is at the heart of the debate and one that he believes can only change if architects 'have their hands on the levers of control'.[1] Like others we have interviewed, Smart describes himself as an architect even though he is acting full-time as a developer: 'We look like a normal office if you come in here, just like any other architectural practice. So, nothing changes, but then everything changes because obviously we don't have clients, we are the invisible clients in the office. And I suppose what that brings about is a huge amount of self-reliance. So, the skill set is undoubtedly very different.'[2]

What that skill set is we will be discussing in the following eight chapters.

For others the relationship between architecture and development is fluid. Jake Edgley, who develops in London alongside designing private houses for one-off clients (see chapter 6), says, 'One thing I find interesting is all the projects that my practice is best known for are our development projects. You would think the development would make the money whereas the architecture would be all about the design. But actually our design research is done on our own developments because those projects pay for it so when we're acting as architects we're reusing the ideas we developed on our own schemes.'[3]

Architects agree that development, if it is successful, is more profitable than architecture. But that's not difficult. A recently qualified architect is looking at an annual salary of just over £36,000,[4] while a senior architect can be expected to be paid in the region of £50,000.[5] In the UK, this needs to be seen in the context of a housing market that has become out of reach for the young and talented, most markedly in London where the majority of architects are employed. Little wonder that one of the initial motivations for a number of architect developers is building their own home.

This is how the practices of Burd Haward (see chapter 2), Liddicoat & Goldhill (see this chapter) and Mikhail Riches (see chapter 4), amongst others, began their property journey, working at a time when it was still possible to accrue enough capital from architectural work and renovations to buy land in London for cash. The property market was buoyant and as David Mikhail remarked, 'It was difficult really to go wrong.'[6] Those days may be over but property can still yield significant profits for architects who have clear objectives and have done their homework, starting with the all-important development appraisal discussed in chapter 2.

For Dutch architect developers Tim Vermeend and Dennis Hauer, their property knowledge was honed during the financial crash when, faced with no work, they advised investors how to develop empty properties above shops in return for a share of the profit. Hauer says, 'Bit by bit, this model developed into where we are now, where we have bank funders and investors, and we do much bigger developments. It allows us to do the architecture we want and build equity and cash in the development side.'[7]

That said, for many architects describing themselves as a 'developer' comes with a red warning light. Hauer is more candid: 'We don't want to be seen as developers as the word has negative connotations due to the lack of trust people have. But it does allow us to build the innovative projects we want, which are highly environmentally friendly buildings that we wouldn't be able to do if we didn't have a financial stake in the development arm.'[8]

But taking control comes with its own risks and we have chosen to speak to architects who, on the whole, have been successful. We have not spoken to the ones who have gone bankrupt in the process, which happens all the time in development. Auctions are full of projects that are in the hands of the receiver because someone came unstuck. It could be because of planning, or the construction costs went over budget. It could also be because the site was mired in red tape (something we will talk more about in chapter 3) or the lenders went bust.

All these things can and do happen so if profit is the only motive for your first project maybe think again. As emphasised through the following chapters, development is not for the faint-hearted; it is a complex journey full of risk, and those who set out without taking this into account are more likely to fail. So, if this is your first project, see it as a steep learning curve and a chance to get you that important track record and some valuable contacts; making money should be the priority for project number two.[9]

CASE STUDY

PROJECT	Printworks, Margate, UK
ARCHITECT DEVELOPER	Liddicoat & Goldhill
DATE	Ongoing

Sophie Goldhill co-founded architecture and interior design studio Liddicoat & Goldhill with her husband David Liddicoat in 2010.[10] Their first development was their own home in Camden, north London, followed by a house in Hackney, east London, also for themselves. In 2017 they bought a former printworks in Margate, Kent as a development site.

The nineteenth-century Printworks had more recently been used as a doctors' surgery. The architects were quick to spot its potential to become their new studio as well as a variety of spaces that they would be able to let to Margate's burgeoning creative community. The outstanding aspects were the beautiful Victorian brick facade and the wonderful original features hidden underneath the ceiling tiles.

They bought the site after seeing a 'For Sale' sign go up on the surgery. Having already lost out on one site in the town they were determined not to lose out a second time. 'We telephoned the agent straight away and said, "Whatever it is, we're going to buy it."' They knew that Tracey Emin and art dealer Carl Freedman had recently bought a big chunk of the building opposite, which wasn't public knowledge at that stage, so they knew that it was a great spot.

Goldhill emphasises the value of being on the ground and looking to the long-term: 'When we bought the Printworks, it wasn't for us to flip in five years; it was a 10- to 15-year horizon, perhaps even longer.' Even though they didn't have a plan of what to do with the space, they set up meetings with local business owners to understand the kind of rent they would be willing to pay. 'Word got around as it's a small town and the creative community is quite tight,' says Goldhill.

And because a concerted effort is being made to help seaside towns via grant aid, there were grants available from the county council, both for the development and also to support the tenants. 'We found that actually there's lots of money floating around if you're starting something new and if you're creating jobs,' says Goldhill.

About a year later, a plot of land came up behind the Printworks. Developers had converted one of the buildings, a listed Post Office building, into flats and a restaurant but demolished the Sorting Office. 'We decided to approach them off-market to buy the land because we just didn't want another development to go on behind us.'

Having purchased this additional site they then spent more than a year working out what they could do with it. In the end they decided to convert part of the Printworks into residential, using the extra land for the commercial space. This includes their own practice, which will be housed in a new building.

Figure 1.1 Liddicoat & Goldhill, Printworks, Margate, Kent. The building dates from around 1870 and was built by the proprietor of the *Isle of Thanet Gazette* as the printing works for his paper. It is located in the heart of Margate's new Arts District.

Like architect George Ferguson, who developed Bristol's Tobacco Factory over many years (see Chapter 6), the Printworks is a classic example of slow development, which is also partly a lifestyle choice. They have been able to take a more relaxed approach to this project because they had already successfully developed in London and used the proceeds from their second house to fund the purchase of the Printworks site.

Goldhill sums up, 'We want to try and enjoy [it]. If we were just about making money, then it would be about selling. But for us, we enjoy doing the projects ... It's a way to diversify our business, which is fundamentally architecture, but the more diverse your portfolio can be, the less of a worry it is when things don't go according to plan. For example, if the houses don't work as rentals, I can just sell them. And because I'm doing it in a phased fashion it doesn't feel like too scary a thing to do.'

Figure 1.2 (above) Liddicoat & Goldhill, Printworks, Margate, Kent. The cafe space serves the residents who include architects, filmmakers, stylists and musicians.

Figure 1.3 (below) Liddicoat & Goldhill, Printworks, Margate, Kent. Having long-term horizons is essential for this project, which is a combination of new-build, renovation, commercial and residential. The architects have planning permission for two new houses in the converted Printworks, extending out the commercial aspect and retaining the cafe.

Figure 1.4 (above) Liddicoat & Goldhill, Printworks, Margate, Kent. The project received public funding because the development is helping to create local employment.

Figure 1.5 (below) Liddicoat & Goldhill, Printworks, Margate, Kent. Roof-terrace cafe.

CHAPTER 2

THE DEVELOPMENT APPRAISAL

In some respects, property is no different to any other industry that needs to work out costs, revenue and return on investment. Except that in property, the uncertainty is so much greater because when you come across a site in an auction catalogue, you have to make assumptions about a long time in the future that are highly unlikely to be accurate six months down the road, let alone three to five years later.

It would be best to think of property development as a journey. You think you know where you're going and the general direction but the reality is that most of the time you have no idea what's around the corner. Bit by bit, as you get closer to the end, you can see where you're going. But in order to complete the project you have to be prepared to live with uncertainty.

This is why the development appraisal is so essential; it gives you some structure from which you can make assumptions, or at least realise what you don't know, and that should give a little clarity before you start the journey. The uncertainty is also the reason why you should be wary of committing time and money unless your profit margin is between 20% and 25%.

Let's imagine you have found your ideal site and it is coming up at auction in two weeks' time. It fits all of your requirements in terms of size and location. Your quick, back-of-the-envelope exercise suggests that with some clever design you could easily build five flats. The guide price is £500,000. However, until you have done an appraisal you can't know whether the site is wildly overvalued or, if your costs are broadly correct, it will deliver you a 25% profit.

Remember your appraisal is just a tool. You are responsible for the inputs and it is the accuracy of these inputs that will determine whether the development will be profitable or not. This means that the more you can find out about the site and the more detail you can put into your appraisal at the outset, the better position you will be in. Always believe in your numbers and don't get swayed by anyone else's appraisal (unless there's something in there that you've forgotten or under-budgeted for) and always be prepared to walk away if the numbers are not adding up.

For example, is there something you have discovered that could significantly derail your costs? Have you seen something which no one else has? It could be something fairly simple, for example a hidden drain you have spotted that will cost £50,000 to move and other bidders have missed it, or it could be a piece of new or imminent legislation that is likely to make planning quicker and easier, which gives you a competitive advantage and allows you to bid higher. Either way, you need to know as much as you can before you start so your costs and your revenue forecasts are as accurate as they can be.

LEARNING THE LINGO

In property, just as in architecture, there is a great deal of jargon, which can cloud the process. Most of the common terms refer to financial calculations, or 'rules of thumb', that you'd be advised to learn before you get started as they crop up all the time.

The most common ones are:

GROSS DEVELOPMENT VALUE (GDV)

GDV is simply the expected value of the whole development once built out.

Example: *If the development is for two homes worth £750,000 and £500,000 respectively, the GDV is £1,250,000. If the development is for a block of five flats each worth £200,000 with 1,000ft² of offices underneath, which should rent at £12.50 per ft², then even if you are intending to keep the office space for yourself the GDV is the value of both the flats and the office space. In this example it would be £200,000 x 5 + the value of the office space if you sold it (say £250,000) = £1,250,000.*

PROFIT ON COST (POC)

This is your total profit divided by your total cost. Confusingly, this can also sometimes be known as your profit margin even though in other industries your profit margin is a percentage of profit against revenue, not against cost.

There's a general rule of thumb in development that you should be aiming for between 20% and 25% as a PoC. The required PoC will mainly depend on the risks you face, for example where you are in the market cycle or whether you have planning permission and who is funding the development. Third-party investors will require 25–30% but you may be happy with 15% if it's all your money.

Example: *If the expected GDV is £1,250,000 and expected costs are £1,000,000, then the expected profit is £250,000. The profit on cost is profit divided by cost (£250,000 divided by £1,000,000), which is 25%.*

A project which involves buying a site, winning planning permission and then building out would normally require a 25% profit margin due to the significant risks involved in planning, construction and the time of the project. Compare this to a simple refurbishment project; in this case, the developer may be happy to proceed on a 10–15% profit margin as there is no planning risk and the construction and time of the project are quicker and less uncertain.

INTERNAL RATE OF RETURN (IRR)

In essence, IRR measures your return over the life of the project taking time into account. Not many people know what IRR means technically, but for completeness it is defined as the discount rate that makes the Net Present Value of all cash flows (both positive and negative) over the course of a project equal to zero.

It is probably easiest to think of it as the average annual (compounding) interest rate a project will pay out over the course of the project's life. Think of putting £100 into a bank and getting a 2% interest rate on it:

Year (start of)	Interest paid	Bank balance
0	£0	£100
1	£2	£102
2	£2.04	£104.04
10	£2.44	£121.90

Table 2.1 Average annual interest rate over the life of a project.

In year one you make £2 interest; year two, you get 2% of £102, i.e. £2.04. After 10 years, you would have £121.90 in the bank.

If you then closed your account and withdrew your money, you would have had an IRR of 2% on your money.

In practice, investors use IRR as a way of comparing completely different projects, some that require them to lock up money for a long time and some that will be quicker. If you do want to work out IRR then it's best to use the built-in formula in Excel.

Example: *Using the same example project above, it takes exactly 3 years with £300,000 invested at the beginning and £450,000 paid back to the investors at the end. The IRR would be approximately 14.5%. Broken down it looks like this:*

Day 0
Investor puts in £300,000
Year 1 (Day 365)
Investor is 'owed' £300,000 + 14.5% in interest = £344,000
Year 2 (Day 730)
Investor is 'owed' £344,000 + 14.5% in interest = £393,000
Year 3 (Day 1,095)
Investor is 'owed' £393,000 + 14.5% in interest = £450,000

RETURN ON INVESTMENT (ROI)

This refers to the money that an investor will get back from each £1 they invest into your project without taking time into account. A rule of thumb is that investors will be seeking a profit of between 40% and 50% on their initial investment on a new-build, ground-up development. Note that ROI does not make any reference to how long a project takes.[1] While it is a simple enough measure to understand, investors tend to prefer IRR as it allows them to more easily compare projects.

Example: *Continuing with the same project example as above, where costs are £1,000,000, if an investor invested £300,000 (the rest coming from other sources) they would normally expect to get back in the region of £450,000 at the end of the project. This would result in a return of £150,000 and a ROI of 50% (£150,000 divided by £300,000).*

RED BOOK VALUATION

A 'Red Book' valuation is an official valuation carried out by a third-party independent surveyor to establish the value of the land or building you are buying. Banks will use this valuation (not yours) to establish what your project is worth and to determine how much they will lend to you. It will also determine how much you have to sell the homes for, so it's an important document and one we will come back to.

The term 'red book' is in theory supposed to follow certain rules to establish a level playing field between different projects and different surveyors, but there is always a degree of subjectivity. This is a very important document for your funding because a low valuation may mean the bank will lend you less money and this may increase the chance of your cash running out, spelling disaster for you and the project. So even though it is expensive, it's sometimes worth getting more than one valuation from different firms.

EQUITY

Equity is the value of the asset (or project) minus any debt outstanding. In other words, equity is what's left once all lenders have been paid off. It effectively represents the 'shareholders' in the project. Normally, but not always, this means that they share in the profit of the project. Normally this will be your share of the profit along with any other investors who have invested money rather than lent money.

DEBT

Debt is the value of all loans and normally, but not always, means that there is an interest rate associated with the debt. We will go into this in greater depth in chapter 5.

Example: *Using the same project example as above, if investors invest £300,000, you invest £50,000 and a bank lends you £650,000 then the equity is £300,000 + £50,000 = £350,000 and the debt is £650,000.*

DOING THE DEVELOPMENT APPRAISAL

In terms of doing a development appraisal, Excel is the best tool as it gives you the greatest flexibility. If your Excel skills are lacking, think about doing an Excel course or buying or accessing one of the many ready-made software packages.

WHAT DOES AN APPRAISAL DO?

It doesn't matter which package you use, all appraisals do the same thing. Simply put, an appraisal helps you to establish *your* value of a piece of land or a building before work begins.[2]

Figure 2.1 Burd Haward, Wolsey Mews, Kentish Town, London. External view of the two buildings carefully designed to accommodate different needs and uses.

Figure 2.2 (above) Burd Haward, Wolsey Mews, Kentish Town, London. Adding a basement across the entire site footprint meant project costs went up from the original budget.

Figure 2.3 (below) Burd Haward, Wolsey Mews, Kentish Town, London. Currently the first-floor living space of one house is Burd Haward's studio, while the second house is rented as a family home.

Figure 2.4 (above) Burd Haward, Wolsey Mews, Kentish Town, London. Before the auction, the architects calculated how much they could build on the site and what that would cost. They then looked at square footage prices in the area.

Figure 2.5 (below) Burd Haward, Wolsey Mews, Kentish Town, London. The terrace from the back of the mews.

Figure 2.6 Burd Haward, Wolsey Mews, Kentish Town, London. The material palette is understated and economic with robust, sustainable, self-finished materials throughout.

Figure 2.7 Burd Haward, Wolsey Mews, Kentish Town, London. Internal staircase to the basement.

CASE STUDY

PROJECT	Ballam Road Apartments, Lytham St Annes, UK
ARCHITECT DEVELOPER	Harrison Hunt
DATE	2019

Diana Borland and James Sanderson founded development company Harrison Hunt and the architectural practice Sanderson Borland in 2017. Their first project was a series of eight apartments in Lytham St Annes, Lancashire, which were developed as a joint venture with the site owners. Their latest project for 34 houses on the west coast of Scotland is now on site with phase one of nine houses. Their story highlights some of the potential pitfalls of developing without any capital.

Borland says development was always something she had been interested in. 'There's a lot of fulfilment from the architectural projects but then you pass off the baby once you've done it. I like to be a bit more in control of my own destiny.'[5]

Sanderson found the site in Lancashire after driving around the area. Although it had an existing property on it, the house had been on the market for a few years. Sanderson knocked on their door, introduced himself and explained what he and Borland were looking to do and asked whether they'd be interested in a joint venture.

With no personal finance or capital, they persuaded the owners of the property to come in with them as development partners. The deal structure was straightforward: the owners put up their house, and the architects put in the sweat equity. They agreed a percentage uplift at the end of the development. A further percentage increase was agreed if the architect developers exceeded what they thought they would achieve in values.

They then had to find the finance to fund the development, which was less easy. Borland explains that 'the price of the build was quite expensive because it was a high-spec building. A broker pitched our story to United Trust Bank and, with some ducking and diving, we managed to get the finance, but they were only prepared to lend us £600,000 of the £1,000,000 we needed, so for the remainder we used crowdfunding.'[6]

A sting in the tail was the 18% interest on the loan. This is because without significant capital to put in as the developer, funders often take the view that you're not putting your bit on the table, says Borland. 'We say, "We're putting in the sweat equity. We get the planning permissions. If you put time against money, we have probably spent £200,000 of our time on the project, trying to get the right funders in place, going back and forth with the planners, building warrants and all of that. So that's the struggle."'

Figure 2.8 Harrison Hunt, Ballam Road, Lytham St Annes. The project earned good architectural fees and helped to establish the practice, which they launched at the same time as the development business.

Although more profit was anticipated at the end, Borland admits she was naive. 'I didn't understand the financing and the funding that would be needed and the eye-watering interest rates ... We've had to get a tougher skin.' However, the result is they got a track record and, from their perspective, they had the architectural fees to help get the practice going as well.

Figure 2.9 (above) Harrison Hunt, Ballam Road, Lytham St Annes. The architects persuaded the planners to allow multiple apartments while paying homage to the art deco style of the original house.

Figure 2.10 (below) Harrison Hunt, Ballam Road, Lytham St Annes. Without cash to put in, the couple entered into a joint venture with the owners of the site who had been trying to sell their home for some time.

CHAPTER 3
RISKS AND HOW TO MANAGE THEM

Risk is everywhere in development. It starts when you purchase the site and ends at a minimum of two years after you have sold the homes or property you have built.

As we've learned, your development appraisal should show a profit of about 20–25% of your total costs; this is the standard industry reward for taking on the risks. Your job as developer is to get the project finished while managing and mitigating the risk. In this chapter we will give you some tips on how to identify the main risks and what to do about them.

If you are an architect, you will likely understand risk in terms of the advice that you give to clients, but as an architect developer you are responsible. This is something that Carl Turner found out when he had to sell his house in order to fund the Pop Brixton project (see chapter 7). Turner's view is that 'you need to risk what you can afford to lose', but that often means convincing others to come on the journey with you.[1] Turner explains, 'I felt at the time that if we'd have lost £150,000 it wouldn't have been great, but it wouldn't have affected our lives horrendously. So I had that discussion with Mary [Turner's partner] and said if it all goes horribly wrong, we might not get the money back and is that okay? Because if it isn't, we won't do it.'[2]

This may sound alarming, even frightening, but the most common reason for projects failing is when the developer has miscalculated risk and runs out of money; that could be caused by anything from not doing enough due diligence (often abbreviated to DD) on the site when you're buying it, underestimating the cost, having an enforcement action served against you by the planners, contractors going bust or the market going into freefall.

Ideally, you will want to deal with risk by understanding as many of the risks as you can, then by mitigating as much of it as possible in advance or by handing it off to someone else – for example, getting a warranty, a fixed-price contract or pre-sales. If that's not possible, you should have a mitigation strategy in place, which is typically an insurance policy. You will be familiar with buildings insurance, but there are many other policies you can consider, including rights to light insurance, rights of way insurance, title indemnity and others that can be useful and pay out in the event of the insured risk happening. You will always encounter things that come up during the project that you hadn't planned for, and this is where your contingency comes into play.

Every project will have its own specific risks and will also have a lot of generic risks that all projects share. Remember, even when people have bought your homes and moved in you're still responsible for sorting out snagging or any other latent defects.

Risk broadly falls under one of the following four main headings:

LEGAL

You will encounter legal risk throughout your property development, but it is normally understandable and quantifiable and mitigated by hiring lawyers or buying insurance. Your lawyer's job is to identify risk for you throughout the process. You do not need to use the same lawyer or firm for each element of the development as some firms specialise in certain aspects. Don't underestimate how much you may end up using a lawyer.

As a minimum you should expect to use a lawyer for the following main activities:

- **buying the land** – checking on title, possession, rights of way, etc.
- **funding the development** – dealing with the bank's lawyers and their due diligence on you and the project
- **selling the properties once built** – dealing with purchasers' lawyers.

However, you may also need or want to use a lawyer to help with:

- **planning** – if, for example, a local authority is causing difficulties, you may need legal advice on the technical side of planning
- **Section 106 agreements** – when negotiating with the local authority
- **rights to light claims, rights of way or adverse possession** – hopefully these are picked up during your due diligence, but they may emerge later in the process
- **construction contracts** – you can use a standard JCT off-the-shelf contract but you may wish to make some amendments to it[3]
- **dispute resolution** – normally with your contractor but in theory it could be with anyone.

You should bear in mind that a lawyer is there to point out all the risks to you and will respond to what you have asked them; they are not always thinking commercially and may point out a risk that is highly unlikely to happen or that will have little impact. It will ultimately be up to you how you quantify the impact, the likelihood of any particular risk happening and what you want to do about it.

PLANNING

The second and probably biggest risk is around planning. In the UK, sites without planning consent are considered highly risky. Generally, they are too risky for a bank to lend against and this is one of the main reasons why builders will rarely buy sites without planning: the associated risk and the time it takes to get planning is just too great. However, planning is a risk that architects understand only too well, which gives them an advantage in negotiating a system that some feel acts as a straitjacket on development.[4]

Of course, with the recent UK planning reforms and permitted development rights (PDR), architects are in a strong position to know what current legislation will allow without any planning risk. The obvious one is still converting commercial to residential, but all planning changes give rise to new opportunities, so it pays to be ahead of the game. Make sure you understand local plans as they include the strategy for housing and other development over the next decade.

There are many businesses in the UK which deal specifically with sourcing land without planning, obtaining a satisfactory planning consent and then selling the sites on. This can be an extremely profitable business as the value of land can often increase by between 50% and 100% of pre-planning values. It is also a business that architect developers can get involved in to build up their capital and utilise their skill set. There are clever ways to ensure you don't have to spend too much money, which we'll talk about in a later chapter 6.

Apart from buying sites with planning permission already in place, there is no easy mitigation strategy for planning risk except to hire a planning consultant to advise you on the chance of success.

CONSTRUCTION

The third major risk is construction. Architects will be familiar with a scenario where construction has been put on hold for two or three years while archaeological work is carried out. Or they may have experienced a contractor going bust, leaving the developer to find a new contractor, sort out the paperwork and reassure the funders that the building will still be built on time and on budget (it rarely will after an event like contractor bankruptcy).

Some of the traditional ways to mitigate against construction risk is to utilise contracts that put the construction risk on the contractor. A design and build (D&B) contract aims to do exactly that, although what you may gain in terms of certainty you can lose in terms of control – and the 'design' element can often be left wanting. Even then, it doesn't always protect you when things go catastrophically wrong financially. If a contractor goes bust, the cost protection of a D&B contract will be worthless.

As is the case with all these risks, there are various ways to mitigate them, but every mitigation measure generally costs money and it is your job as a developer to decide which risks to mitigate and how much to spend.

THE MARKET

The final pillar of risk is around the market itself. This is because you may be buying a site – especially if it is a site without planning – many years before you are going to start selling it. With the time a development project takes there is always a possibility that the completed development gets delivered to the market in a downturn. Big developers will always try to mitigate this by selling off-plan and there's nothing stopping you doing the same.

It's generally acknowledged that buyers committing early to a scheme will require a discount, and so it's up to you to decide how much discount you are prepared to give for sales certainty. For any development greater than five units, selling around half of the units in any development before it is completed and comes to the market is a good rule of thumb. We'll also cover other strategies around marketing and sales in chapter 8.

RISK REGISTERS

The right way to capture risk is to set up a risk register using a simple Excel spreadsheet. It is usually created at the start of the project, once you have completed planning and are starting to look at construction, and should be reviewed on a regular, monthly basis. However, you can just as easily set one up as soon as you have spotted a site, or once you have bought a site and are seeking planning permission.

You should ask your professional team to add any risks that they see to the project along with how to mitigate them. What you are trying to do is to assess each risk in turn for the likelihood of it happening and the impact it will have on the project. Take each risk, calculate out of 10 the likelihood (10 being highly likely) and the impact (10 being highly impactful) and then multiply the number. This will give you the key risks to look at (say anything with a score of greater than 10) and you should have a mitigation strategy for each risk.

For example, the chance of the building being burnt down may be 1 out of 10, whilst the impact is 10 out of 10, giving it a score of 1 x 10 = 10. Mitigation strategy: insurance.

The table below shows a typical risk register template for a project with a few lines filled in. You can choose to do a risk register for each stage of the project, or you can do a comprehensive one at the start. Follow the four main pillars of risk as set out on the previous pages and work with your team of advisers to fill out the table. At the beginning of a project, this will have many hundreds of lines depending on how detailed you want to be, but as you go through the project they will gradually disappear until you have no more exposure to risk.

Issue	Consequence	Likelihood	Impact	Overall severity	Risk mitigation strategy	Risk owner
		Low 1–3 Medium 4–6 High 7–10	Low 1–3 Medium 4–6 High 7–10	Likelihood x Impact		
Failure to start on site within 3 years of consent	Loss of planning permission	1	10	10	Main contractor to start excavation on site prior to main works	PM
Contractor goes bust	Impact on time and budget of project	2	7	14	Examine financial resilience of contractor and continue to monitor. Get performance bond or increase retention	QS
Project overspend	Run out of money, bank stops funding	3	8	24	Use D&B or fixed-price contract	QS
Building burns down	Delay to construction	1	10	10	Buy insurance, ensure contractor has insurance	PM
Slow sales	Risk of bank asking for money back	5	7	35	Sell 50% of project off-plan. Rent out remaining units	Developer

Table 3.1 Risk register template

CASE STUDY

PROJECT	Carpenters Row, London, UK
ARCHITECT DEVELOPER	ByOthers
DATE	Ongoing

Richard Keys founded London-based practice ByOthers in 2020. His first development project is a housing scheme in south London comprising of nine timber-clad, three-bedroom houses.

The way he came to acquire the 0.18ha site is complex, highlighting the risks that come with purchasing land. Keys explains, 'I had seen a piece of land near to where I was living that was heavily overgrown. It had fly tipping on it, Japanese knotweed and people were also using it for illegal garden grabbing. I thought this looked like a tricky site, but it also looked like a site that could be developed.'[5]

The story that follows is almost Dickensian, but it's one that is still very relevant today. While he was trying to track down the owner via the Land Registry he met a woman who had acquired a portion of the site through adverse possession and was planning to build a house.[6] Shortly after she submitted her application she was contacted by an 'heir hunter' who informed her that he had tracked down the rightful heirs to the land, so she would need to hand back the land immediately. If she did not, she would be taken to court.

Keys says, 'At that point I laughed because I'd seen title deeds, which had my acquaintance's [the woman's] name on it. So, I said, "I don't think you should just hand this back," because she'd done the legwork in trying to get planning permission and, even though it was refused, she was proposing to go back and address all the issues.'

However, his advice was overtaken by events. The 'heir hunter' filed a claim to the courts on the basis that the original owner, who was deceased, had left the land in trust to her daughter. There is a quirk in English law that says if land is owned by a trust there is an exclusion for adverse possession claims, so his acquaintance's right to the land was invalid.

Unfortunately for Keys' acquaintance, she had claimed land under adverse possession that she shouldn't have been able to claim and was taken to court, lost the court case and lost the land. At that point, knowing the land much better than the landowner did, Keys picked up the phone to the other side and said he was interested in buying the land, which ultimately led to an agreement.

Having witnessed a court case where land was taken off someone who had a Land Registry title, he was understandably concerned that the level of due diligence he needed to do had to go beyond what was simply noted on the Land Registry title. But is all this really necessary?

Figure 3.1 ByOthers, Carpenters Row, West Norwood, London. The urban backland site is bound by a railway line and terraced flats. The scheme is for nine family homes, arranged as a broken terrace along the southern edge of the site.

In most cases, the title on the Land Registry will be correct and if there are any issues with title they will be uncovered, as long as you carry out extensive due diligence – so his acquaintance's right to the land was invalid. If you are buying land at auction the risks are much higher because you do not have the time to do the due diligence, bearing in mind that requesting documents from the Land Registry can take months.

Keys says, 'The misconception is that your lawyer will do all sorts of due diligence for you and they will cover absolutely every base. The reality is that law firms don't see risk in the same way that architects do. They do a level of due diligence that can and will miss things – and as a property purchaser you are ultimately responsible.'

When you're dealing with a site like this one with adverse possession, a deceased owner, fly tipping and issues with the Land Registry title, being able to communicate the information to

Figure 3.2 ByOthers, Carpenters Row, West Norwood, London. The scheme features abundant planting, with a garden greeting residents before they walk along an elevated, shared walkway.

your legal team is key. It's important to remember that the legal team almost never visits sites, so you are their eyes and ears. Photographs and documentation are key to helping your lawyers understand what is happening on site.

Keys and his legal team made many requests to the Land Registry for prior transfers, going back 150 years up to the stage of the deceased owner, in order to establish the history of the site and to access information.[7]

Although the due diligence didn't uncover anything abnormal, when someone else approached him to claim adverse possession, he was able to show the full history of the land. He concludes, 'We even spoke to solicitors who did transfers 70 years ago. So, the key here is when you come to a tricky piece of land, which has, in this sense, been completely abandoned, you must go into all of the detail and do [a high] level of due diligence.'

CASE STUDY	
PROJECT	Nightingale 1, Brunswick, Melbourne, Australia
ARCHITECT DEVELOPER	Breathe Architecture
DATE	2017

Jeremy McLeod is the founder of Breathe Architecture and the developer of Nightingale 1, an apartment building in Melbourne's Brunswick district. After completing Nightingale in 2017, he set up Nightingale Housing, a not-for-profit housing provider working across four states in Australia.

He conceived his first development, The Commons, in 2007 with an ambition to create Australia's first 'car-free, carbon-free building – a sustainable flagship building that would set a precedent'.[8] The project was taken over by an ethical developer, Small Giants, due to changing market conditions caused by the global financial crash. McLeod explains, 'We used The Commons as a prototype to start to educate the market and invited every developer in the city to come and see it. But after about two years, no developer called us and said, "This is great, can you do that again?" They saw it as a blip on the radar, rather than a trend, while we saw it as massive latent demand.'

Figure 3.3 Breathe Architecture, Nightingale 1, Brunswick, Melbourne. Nightingale was born from the conviction that people deserve affordable, well-designed homes that encourage communal living.

Figure 3.4 Breathe Architecture, Nightingale 1, Brunswick, Melbourne. When owners want to sell, they must offer their property to the waiting list price capped to match the overall property price increases in the locality.

Figure 3.5 Breathe Architecture, Nightingale 1, Brunswick, Melbourne. It is the country's first residential building to be connected under an embedded network that is 100% fossil fuel free.

In spring 2015, McLeod bought a former industrial site diagonally opposite The Commons with a A$50,000 deposit and a lot of risk, that included having to find the money and secure shareholders over a 90-day period. He elaborates, 'We essentially door-knocked every architect I knew in the city, all of our friends and family, to find 27 shareholders to put in A$100,000 each. In fact, we only needed 22 because my partner Tamara and I agreed to mortgage our home so we could buy the first five shares. We literally bet our house on it and said to everyone, "We can't afford for this to fail because we will lose everything." We got some of the city's best architects to invest in it and we told them that we would share the IP with them and teach them how to do what we were doing.'

McLeod was granted a planning permit for 20 apartments, three tiny retail spaces and various rooftop amenities including a laundry, vegetable patch and a communal dining and garden area. A contractor had agreed to build the development for A$6,000,000 and at the same time the ballot for the apartments opened and all of them sold.

Three weeks later, he received an objection from the developer next door who took him to an appeals tribunal because there was no car parking in the proposed development. The appeal was upheld and McLeod was forced to put in three shared car spaces and take out 30 bike spaces as a result. McLeod says, 'It was insane. The local media started writing articles about the planning decision and then we started receiving calls from a few planning lawyers saying, "This is ridiculous, let us help you fight it."'

At the council meeting to review the decision 400 people wrote to support the planning application and McLeod had a collection of planning and legal experts who were prepared to represent him probono. Having overcome this hurdle – which had delayed the project by eight months – there was a further amendment to the scheme following a fire in the city's docklands and the Grenfell Tower fire in London which led to a change to the building regulations. The plan to use timber for the outside of the building had to be scrapped.

Altogether the appeals tribunal and change of materials to concrete and steel added A$540,000 to the project. McLeod explains, 'We had to go back to all of our residents and say, "We're really sorry but you have two choices: you can either pay more for your apartment to cover the additional costs, or you can walk away from your contract." Of the 20 purchasers 18 stayed on.'

The final hurdle was securing senior debt. McLeod says, 'We had enough money in our equity position to buy the land and to fund the development through to construction, but we needed A$6,000,000 in debt from the bank to build it. We didn't want to take money from any of the big four banks here [in Australia] because of their fossil fuel lending. Over the course of six months I met with 34 banks, mutuals and credit societies to secure senior debt.'

In the end, an impact investment group in Sydney, Social Enterprise Finance Australia (SEFA), saw The Commons and what the developers were trying to do and, as McLeod says, 'They basically willed it into existence and built a lending syndicate with a couple of high-net-worth individuals that put in A$1,000,000 each and lent that money back to us at 6%.'

Figure 3.6 Breathe Architecture, The Commons, Brunswick, Melbourne. Opposite Nightingale 1 on Florence Street sits The Commons, the precursor to Nightingale 1.

Nightingale Housing delivered all the equity investors a fixed 15% return per annum. With the money in the bank, they paid out their tax liabilities and anything else owed and then wrapped up the lending syndicate. What set them apart from standard developers was that the A$109,000 left over after paying back SEFA and the investors was given back to the residents.

McLeod concludes by saying, 'Developers have worked out that if they're going to sell in and around the inner north of Melbourne, they need to match Nightingale's sustainability credentials, and that is awesome. We're not arrogant enough to think that we can solve the problem for 116,000 people experiencing homelessness, or we can build enough housing to actually solve for climate change. But we do think that we can affect market change and that's our goal.'

Figure 3.7 (above) Breathe Architecture, Nightingale 1, Brunswick, Melbourne. Around 20% of units are set aside for 'priority allocation', including Indigenous people and key workers.

Figure 3.8 (below) Breathe Architecture, Nightingale 1, Brunswick, Melbourne. A typical apartment kitchen and dining space.

Figure 3.9 (above) Breathe Architecture, Nightingale 1, Brunswick, Melbourne. The architects adopted an honest material palette with an emphasis on reduction.

Figure 3.10 (below) Breathe Architecture, Nightingale 1, Brunswick, Melbourne. The entrance to Nightingale 1.

CHAPTER 4
HOW TO FIND LAND

As Mark Twain famously once said, 'Buy land! They're not making it anymore.' But how and where do you find that potentially lucrative prospect of land – the primary requisite to becoming a successful developer in today's world – with the minimum risk of losing your money?

We will come on to the different routes to finding land, but walk around any major city and you will see plenty of infill sites that could be built on. Maybe you've even researched sites you've spotted, or registered with specialist agents and scoured the auctions for opportunities. Finding the land is not the hard part, it's finding land that is both available for sale and being sold at the right price that gives you your 20–25% profit.

In the UK it is not impossible to buy land off a public body but it is very difficult.[1] Not-for-profit developer Naked House was established by four young Londoners in 2013 who couldn't afford to buy and were uninspired by increasingly expensive shared-ownership flats. Although they now have planning permission and funding to build 22 affordable homes, it took Naked House almost nine years to come to an agreement with the local authority on how the deal would work.

Our tip is to diversify your efforts. Don't spend all of your time chasing a site in public ownership. Spend some time writing letters to private landowners – an approach adopted by John Smart – and talk to people – there is nothing to beat word of mouth, as Sophie Goldhill and David Liddicoat found when they were buying a site in Margate (see chapter 1).

Architect developers who were lucky enough to buy their first site before the economic crash of 2008 will complain that in cities, including London and New York, land is now too expensive and there is nothing left to buy. This is untrue. There is always land and there are always new opportunities. As an architect you are uniquely placed to use your skill in spotting the sites that can be fundamentally changed through good design.

THE THREE ROUTES TO FINDING LAND

There are three main routes to purchasing land and they each have their pros and cons:

- **'on-market'** – for all the world to see via estate agents, auctions and online
- **'pre-market'** – where the land agent is offering the land to you and a few others, thus competitively, but not publicly
- **'off-market'** – when there is potentially only you negotiating directly with the landowner.

ON-MARKET LAND

There are two main routes to buying 'on-market' land. The auction route or the standard sale route (sometimes referred to as 'private treaty sale').

Private Treaty

The key to sourcing and buying land under private treaty is to understand it from the view of the estate agents, who prefer to do the deal as quickly and efficiently as possible with minimum work for maximum return. It is therefore important to make agents realise that you are a serious and informed buyer and you have the money. Once you have built trust and credibility, agents will ensure that you are on the list to see new sites as they come up for sale.

Let's imagine an onion, representing layers of people. The outer layer is all those people who see an advert on Rightmove, for example. They are often referred to as 'tyre-kickers', with no development track record or cash to make the purchase.

However, the inner core of the onion represents the people who the agent will go to first and is no more than a handful of developers they know and trust to buy and to deliver. These developers may only buy a handful of sites a year, but they are reliable. The agents know that if they make an offer they're not going to try to reduce the price later, known as 'chipping', nor are they going to cause them any embarrassment with their client. So you want to be as close to that inner core of the onion as you can be.

So how do you become part of the inner core? To begin with, it is about networking, building relationships with estate agents and making sure that they know you're for real. They need to understand what you want, that you are motivated and not a time-waster and crucially that you have the money. One way to incentivise agents, for example, is by offering to pay them a finder's fee so they come to you before going to anyone else. A typical finder's fee will be between 1% and 2% of the purchase price.

Another way to incentivise the agent is to offer them the commission to sell the homes once they are built. For an estate agent, that's a double win: they get the commission on the land and on the homes. In fact, this is so common it's become a condition of business for some agents.

So, what are the pros and cons of going through an estate agent and finding land 'on-market'?

A major advantage is that if it's on the market with an estate agent then there's a good chance that the landowner is ready to sell. Be aware, however, that some landowners will put land on the market just to see what it's worth with no real intention of selling. That's unlikely to happen with bigger agents, but it frequently occurs with the smaller ones.

'On-market' land is generally a quicker deal because the landowner will have already instructed lawyers and be in a position where they are ready to sell. Another advantage is that as the buyer you will generally have time to do lots of due diligence.

That said, a big disadvantage will be the competition because with 'on-market' land everyone can see it. There is also a strong likelihood, because you are on the outer layer of the onion, that other developers have already seen the site and rejected it. It is important to ask yourself: if I like this site, why does no one else? What am I missing here?

It may look like a perfectly good site but is it too expensive for the numbers to stack up? This is very common – the majority of developers will reject 90–95% of sites as overpriced, but agents keep them on the market in the hope that an inexperienced buyer without a proper development appraisal will be foolish enough to part with their cash. Overpriced land can sometimes take a long time to sell. Landowners are initially seduced by the promise of large numbers by agents who hope to sell the land to the greater fool.[2] However, fairly often, overpriced land doesn't sell, and the landowner will either continue to hold on with the hope that values will go up or, occasionally, will end up reducing the price. One of the issues with the land market is that unless a landowner has borrowed money against land (which tends to be rare) it is relatively cheap to hold. Unfortunately, this means that if there is a large price correction it rarely results in lots of land becoming available to buy cheaply.

So don't be afraid of bidding on land that's been on the market for a long time because there may be genuine reasons why its price has dropped. This could be because an agent has over-valued the site because he or she thought it would be possible to get many more homes on it than is actually possible. You could find that, several years later, a site that was originally earmarked for tens or hundreds of homes has been reduced by as much as 90% when it becomes apparent it's only suitable for a development of five houses. In summary, when it comes to open market sale with estate agents, it doesn't mean you can't find land and do deals, it just means you have to be extra cautious – check you haven't missed something either in the site, the title documents or in the numbers.

Yet as an architect, you can often see where a previous planning refusal could be reversed by clever design. Donald Matheson, whose practice Matheson Whitley bought two garages in an east London mews in 2017, knew that the site's previous planning history could put off conventional developers and, therefore, the owner could be more willing to sell. He explained, 'When we went to the open viewing there was a queue of people out the door. But there were aspects of the site that put some straightforward developers off. It was an unadopted road and it had quite a bad planning history. A previous application for residential conversion went to appeal and had been refused. People who might have ordinarily bid on the building didn't want to go ahead with it for those reasons. So, we put a bid in and it was accepted by the owner.'[3]

Property portals

Any prospective developer should also be aware of the property portals, such as Zoopla and Rightmove, while bearing in mind that the portals sit in the outer layer of the onion analogy. Clearly many people will already have seen potentially interesting listings before they end up on Rightmove, but nevertheless, portals are worth keeping an eye on because occasionally you can find good opportunities that others have missed.

Architects have an advantage here because you can potentially see things that other people have overlooked and because other people may be insufficiently aware of the regulations. You can use your skills and expertise to become good land finders. Another good place to look for slightly larger sites is *Estates Gazette*, both in the magazine and online. Most public land sales are either sold through the auctions or via *Estates Gazette*.

Auctions

A good way for a small developer to get started is through auctions, which has always been a popular way to find small sites. The advantage for a newcomer is that you will not be questioned about whether you have the money to buy the site or the necessary experience to deliver. You are given the same information as everyone else so in this respect it's a totally level playing field.

Auctions also provide a good steady stream of sites. Online access to auctioneers is generally free. EIG Auctions, which collates all the auctions throughout the UK, charges an annual fee for access to its powerful database of all past and future auctions, but it also does a lot of the hard work by allowing the user to set up sophisticated search alerts whenever there's land in a specific area or alerts whenever an agent posts a development opportunity.

The main benefit of the auction route is that this is the quickest route to buy land. The primary hazard with auctions, however, is the old phrase *caveat emptor* – or 'buyer beware'. In other words, you must be very sure that what you are buying is something you want to buy and you are not going to end up with a lemon. Should you or your lawyer subsequently uncover something bad or even terrible, you cannot then change your mind or reduce the price. If you really are having second thoughts, you will either have to forfeit your 10% deposit or go through with the deal and try to unravel the problems later.

That said, everyone shares the same risk. In theory, as a result of the short timescales and increased risk of buying at auction, there should be a discount to the price you may pay going via an estate agent and private treaty. The advantage is that it is an open and transparent process; there are no sealed bids, so you don't have to be on the inner core of the onion here.

But of course, it can be very difficult to predict the room (or increasingly the virtual room as more and more auctions are now conducted online). There can be one other bidder who is determined to buy that piece of land for whatever reason, and without becoming an expert in gaming theory, you don't know what they're prepared to bid. So, the best strategy is to set your own price and decide what you are going to bow out at and don't get carried away.

With regards to risk, clearly auctions are the riskiest route you can go down because you have the least amount of time and you need to have your finance in place. Or, at the very least, 10% in cash, because that is what you need on the day to exchange. You will then have between four and eight weeks to find the remaining 90%. However, beware, there have been many occasions when people bid and win the lot and who subsequently lose their 10% because they gamble on raising the finance and fail.

One tip is to check on sites that don't sell in the room. On occasion, sites fail to sell straight away, mainly because they seem difficult. But because they didn't sell, it has taken the pressure away from you as a buyer and, importantly, you have the opportunity to make an offer below the reserve price. If you do buy after the auction, note that you are still buying under auction conditions and will have to put down 10% there and then and complete shortly afterwards.

Public land owners

It's also worth registering with various public land portals. Homes England have a duty to keep them, as do Transport for London, the GLA and various other public bodies. One of the benefits of dealing with local authority or publicly owned land is that the process has to be transparent and you will often find the phrase 'best consideration'. In other words, they must show that they are selling off public goods for the highest price and this is quite often why you will find their land being sold at auction. Sometimes public bodies will attempt to introduce quality into the bidding process, but, because of the pressure for revenue maximisation and the fear of judicial review, they usually have to sell for the highest offer whatever their intention and whatever they tell you.

A positive aspect of land being disposed of by public bodies is that they must market the land to the widest number of people, either through *Estates Gazette* or at auction, both considered open market. Occasionally it is possible to buy land off-market from public authorities, but it is rare and you will have to present a very good argument to be persuasive. Nevertheless, it's worth keeping an eye out for public bodies selling land via their own websites.[4] One can enquire directly, but despite some recent assurances that they would give the 'spotter' first refusal, be aware that they might just thank you and then take it for disposal at auction.

The last thing to note about buying from public bodies is that the process can be extremely lengthy, which is a major disadvantage for short-term investors and can make the process risky and very uncertain.

PRE-MARKET LAND

The second category of land is 'pre-market', which can be thought of as the inner core in our onion analogy. When an agent puts a site on to Rightmove or into *Estates Gazette*, they are often inundated with calls and emails. The vast majority of these are from wannabe developers who don't have the first clue about development. In other words, they are unlikely to raise the money to buy the site and generally just waste the agent's time. The agent stands to make a commission on the land price, so if the land is being offered for say £500,000 and the agent is being paid 2% that's a potential payment of £10,000. The agent wants to minimise the time they spend on the sale to maximise their profit. It therefore makes sense for them to deal with a more exclusive list of tried-and-trusted developers who will be quick to buy the land.

It also makes sense for you to try to be in that inner circle of trusted developers so that you get to find out about all the land deals before they reach the open market. That way, you are competing with five to 10 developers who know what they're doing and do proper development appraisals, rather than 50 to 100 wannabe developers who may over bid or over pay for a site making your reasonable and considered offer look unattractive.

Our tip is to network and connect with estate agents so they can trust and rely on you, and so that they know you have the money. But proving yourself can be a bit of a Catch 22. On the one hand, you need to be in the inner circle to be offered land, on the other hand, you need to buy land to get to the inner circle.

CASE STUDY

PROJECT	The Badge Works, Alben Works, Squirrel Works, Birmingham, UK
ARCHITECT DEVELOPER	Sjölander da Cruz Architects
COMPLETION	The Badge Works 2014; Squirrel Works 2019; Alben Works 2022

Maria Sjölander and Marco da Cruz founded Sjölander da Cruz Architects in 2001. They set up their development company, LIV Projekt, at the same time as their first development, The Badge Works. All developments bar one have been in Birmingham's historic Jewellery Quarter.

The Jewellery Quarter is an urban industrial area with a fascinating history of jewellery and metalware production and a plethora of historic buildings, many of which had been neglected and abandoned. The architects emphasise the importance of knowing the place that you're developing inside out: 'We know every building in the Jewellery Quarter and we know Birmingham city centre almost as well now. We know the developments which are happening and we know the planning approvals that have been given in the past three years. You've got to know your market and what the values are and know the kind of people who are buying.'[5]

The Badge Works became their blueprint for future projects, explains Sjölander: 'We approached Badge Works like we do with all our developments – we started with a sketch design and an appraisal to see what kind of values we could create. When we bought the building, it was 2011 after the financial crash and prices had slumped a bit. It had been on the market for a long time. We bought it at a good price.'

The building had existing planning permission for offices. The architects applied for a new permission for live/work units that traditionally don't achieve the same values as residential, but it was a planning condition set by the council. 'We thought, "What's so bad about live/work?" Actually, it's perfect because that's what everyone wants to do. There was a risk but it sold like hot cakes.'

Having established there was a growing market for contemporary homes, their next development, Squirrel Works, was the conversion of a Grade II listed former silversmith factory into four apartments, one townhouse and a large ground-floor workspace.

Da Cruz explains, 'Squirrel Works already had an atrocious planning approval on it when we bought it. The developer had basically machine-gunned tiny little apartments into it, which should never have been approved because it's a beautiful Arts and Crafts building.'

The architects completely redesigned it and reduced the number of units, having first done an appraisal with the estate agent to ensure they would still make a profit. 'We're not doing this on a wing and prayer, but if you see a building you love and you can see what the potential is you just want to do it', says da Cruz.

Alben Works, their latest development, is also their first new-build, reflecting the very limited supply of the historic buildings once so attainable, and is a significant departure for the couple. 'It was a site that nobody else wanted and it was a difficult site,' explains da Cruz. It had a disused substation at the front and two single-storey, 1960s sheds to the rear of the site, which had once been a badge factory.

The architects' success has been dependent on knowing their area but also knowing their market. Da Cruz's advice is to 'be realistic about what the market will take. It's alright being ambitious and thinking that you can create your own market, but there's got to be a foundation in reality as well, because you can easily create a vanity project that nobody wants. We've always tried not to do that. For all our idealism I think we've always been rooted in reality. You have to be, otherwise you're going to come a cropper.'

Figure 4.1 Sjölander da Cruz Architects, Squirrel Works, Jewellery Quarter, Birmingham. A glass pavilion addition to the top of the building forms the upper floor of the penthouse.

Figure 4.2 Sjölander da Cruz Architects, Squirrel Works, Jewellery Quarter, Birmingham. The former silver factory has been carefully repurposed to deliver a series of apartments topped off with a roof-top penthouse. On the front facade new double-glazed timber windows were installed replicating those of the original building.

Figure 4.3 (above) Sjölander da Cruz Architects, The Badge Works, Jewellery Quarter, Birmingham. Right from the start the architects made a conscious decision to redevelop old industrial buildings that were lying empty and were affordable.

Figure 4.4 (below) Sjölander da Cruz Architects, The Badge Works, Jewellery Quarter, Birmingham. The building before conversion. The original roof was removed to create the courtyard and terraces.

Figure 4.5 Sjölander da Cruz Architects, The Badge Works, Jewellery Quarter, Birmingham. The courtyard space acts as a light well, retaining the memory of the previous industrial use with the adaptation of the existing crane and steel beams.

Figure 4.6 Sjölander da Cruz Architects, Alben Works, Jewellery Quarter, Birmingham. Inspired by the historic typology of the Jewellery Quarter, the nine individual townhouses are a reinterpretation of the Georgian and Victorian terraces that filled the quarter before industrialisation.

Figure 4.7 (above) Sjölander da Cruz Architects, Alben Works, Jewellery Quarter, Birmingham. A typical townhouse accommodates an open-plan kitchen and dining area on the second floor with a double-height light well linking to the living area above.

Figure 4.8 (below) Sjölander da Cruz Architects, Alben Works, Jewellery Quarter, Birmingham. To differentiate themselves from local developers, the architects always stress the integrity of the space and energy efficiency in their marketing.

Figure 4.9 (above) Sjölander da Cruz Architects, Alben Works, Jewellery Quarter, Birmingham. The mixed-use development consists of nine houses arranged around a courtyard, together with live/work lofts and ground-floor commercial space fronting the site.

Figure 4.10 (opposite) Sjölander da Cruz Architects, Alben Works, Jewellery Quarter, Birmingham. The double-height void enables natural light to filter through the spaces and creates a strong connection to the city.

OFF-MARKET LAND

Lastly, we come to 'off-market land', often thought of as the Holy Grail because it's exclusive to the landowner, with little or no competition, so generally cheaper, thus giving you the luxury of a margin that can be spent on design.

Beware though, as direct negotiation with the landowner can take several years to complete. However, this gives plenty of time for checks, due diligence and assessing whether the land is viable or not. It also allows opportunities to negotiate different types of purchase: to buy it unconditionally or subject to planning.[6] This is better for your cash flow because you require less money up front. You might secure the land with an option and put very little money down while you get planning.

While the advantages of off-market land are clear, the question remains: where do you find it?

There are now lots of digital tools to help you find land. You can subscribe to various tech platforms, which identify the owners of buildings and land and allow you to examine the planning history of those sites and then approach the owners. Equally, you can still be successful just walking or cycling around your targeted neighbourhood and looking for opportunities, posting letters through doors or identifying owners on the Land Registry.

Land doesn't always mean a cleared site and could be an existing building, a demolition or a rebuild. It could be a build on top with air space or a subdivide of an existing plot, which is probably the most common way for builders and developers to pick up plots.

Another source of information is the local authorities' own planning portals, which are databases of all planning-related applications. It's easy to register and receive weekly updates on all the planning decisions in the areas that you're interested in. From the portals you can extract information that might lead you to landowners who are interested in selling, maybe because they have failed to win planning permission for a site or have run out of money. Sometimes the owner's details are on there, sometimes it is the architect or planning consultant's details.

Google Maps has been a game changer for looking for sites. You don't have to travel anywhere because you can just do a quick street view and detailed satellite aerial views, even in 3D. You can also use Google to mark sites or make initial measurements if you want to do a quick scheme for your development appraisal.

Street View also allows you to move back in time as well as viewing in the present and is useful for understanding what has happened to the land over the last 10 years. If you want to go back further (which can help with planning), there are old OS plans, which reveal what was there 50, 150 or 200 years ago – key if you need to establish whether there has ever been housing on the site.

Also, don't forget to include other industry-related professionals like contractors among your contacts when scouting for land. Even the local builder's merchant or the pub can be a good source of local knowledge.

Different routes to finding land have been discussed, but a key message remains. Get out there, network, talk to people and most of all, know your neighbourhood.

WHAT TO LOOK FOR WHEN BUYING A SITE

In Table 4.1 we look at some of the issues that can blight a development appraisal that people often overlook. Caution, the list is not exhaustive, and you should always check for site-specific issues. A more comprehensive list of costs is in Appendix A.

Rights to light/existing windows on neighbouring buildings	This is both a civil matter and a planning matter – and it can be very expensive to put right! Don't assume that just because planners have given you the all clear that you are ok. You can pay a consultant to do a model and work out your liability. You can also find some insurance companies that will insure against it.
Party walls	You will need a party wall award for every leaseholder and freeholder. It can get very expensive as you have to pay for both your and their surveyor.
Overlooking	This is a planning issue – some local authorities have 30- and 45-degree angle rules from boundaries and windows so be aware of windows and fences.
Tree preservation orders	You may need to use an arboricultural survey to be certain – or the planners may require you to have one done.
Simple infrastructure	Think about your services: drainage, electricity, water, gas (if needed) – you can get maps of the area from the utility providers.
Japanese knotweed	A major pain – expensive to remove and takes a long time!
Asbestos	Not quite so painful as Japanese knotweed – but still expensive to remove if you have to.
Contaminated land	Is there a chance of contaminated land? If so, what kind of contamination? This can add a lot to your excavation costs depending on the contaminants.
Protected species and ecological constraints	This is more relevant out of city/urban locations but is expensive and can play havoc with programmes as you can only work at certain times of the year.
Slopes and topography	Adds a lot to your foundation costs.
Manholes	Is there a drain or a sewer running through your site? It can be time-consuming and expensive to move or build over.

Substations	Generally not insurmountable, but add a decent budget in time and money for dealing with it.
Overhead cables	Will they interfere with your building or when you are building?
Transport networks	Is there any infrastructure that you need to think about? A railway or a subway? This will add time and cost.
Residents' associations and amenity societies	Active RAs are often against any new development. Consider early consultation.
Access	Don't forget that your development will need to provide basic infrastructure to its residents. For example, where will bins go and will fire and emergency vehicles be able to reach the new homes? Larger or more rural sites will need to consider highways early on too.
Rights of way	If you are buying a backland site you should make sure that you have a right of way to your land. There are insurance policies that can help if the situation is not clear but make sure you get help from a lawyer.

Table 4.1 Things to look for when assessing a site

CASE STUDY

PROJECT	The Old St John's Convent and Orchard, London, UK
ARCHITECT DEVELOPER	Craftworks
COMPLETION	2014

Even as a teenager John Smart was 'dabbling in early business experiments' reinforced, he says, by studying at The Bartlett, where 'you're left to find a site and get on with it'.[7] Starting small, he now has a pipeline of 20 sites, which he is building out: 'We have smaller projects, with a 12- to-18-month timeline, medium-sized sites with maybe a 24-month timeline and then the larger projects, which will take between three to four years.'

But he resists being called an 'architect developer' and explains, 'My focus is on delivering buildings, that's my core purpose, and making those buildings successful. The centrefold activity for us right now is how do we build effectively but also create a unique product – our model really hinges around that. So, I'm not too fussed about what or how we are defined.'

Yet his approach to development is almost forensic. After buying his first site in 2004, he soon discovered that developing one project at a time made him vulnerable to the vagaries of the market. He found that after building a scheme out and making a profit, a recession would come along and it would become about servicing the interest costs.

To try to avoid being exposed to the vagaries of the market, Smart decided to change tactics and took on staff specifically to find sites over a six-month period that he could buy either with options or working with partners.

He says, 'It was a conscious decision to just go hell for leather ... because I knew that if we're just bouncing from one project to the next there was no cream. It was just enough milk to keep us going, but we weren't particularly growing as an entity. So I changed the model where we weren't just kind of going from one project to the next and went into a phase of buying lots of sites.'

It meant that he could spot sites he thought had potential very quickly because he was working with agents but he was also on top of emerging policies and action plans that could impact planning.

On average, he estimates that he had about a 2% response rate from around 25,000 letters that were sent out, and a further 2% acquisition rate from the responses so the odds were extremely low (on average one site bought for every 5,000 letters sent out), but it was a great way to find off-market land.

Smart reflects, 'If I was starting out today, the key would be to look at working with investors. There's a lot more investors out there and the market has really opened up. There could be a more collaborative route going forward, where the investor doesn't have the inclination or skill set to go about finding a site, or to get planning, or to know how to put a team together, and that could be a vehicle to get the seed capital together, because it's very difficult otherwise.'

Figure 4.11 (opposite, above) Craftworks, The Old St John's Convent and Orchard, Camberwell, London. An existing Victorian convent was converted to create four five-storey houses.

Figure 4.12 (opposite, below) Craftworks, The Old St John's Convent and Orchard, Camberwell, London. The oak staircase was constructed using staves of standard section sizes that were laminated into a bespoke form.

Figure 4.13 (below) Craftworks, The Old St John's Convent and Orchard, London. Each house is designed as a series of cloistered spaces, punctuated by opne-plan and double-height spaces.

Figure 4.14 (above) Craftworks, The Old St John's Convent and Orchard, Camberwell, London. Each house is set over five floors and spans over 4,000ft².

Figure 4.15 (below) Craftworks, The Old St John's Convent and Orchard, Camberwell, London. The practice used its own team of builders for the project and is keen to see if it can revive the role of the architect as 'master craftsman'.

CASE STUDY

PROJECT	Church Walk, London, UK
ARCHITECT DEVELOPER	Mikhail Riches
COMPLETION	2013

Annalie Riches and David Mikhail bought their site at auction in 2007. The development in Hackney, east London, consists of two houses, a flat and a triplex. Church Walk won the RIBA's London Building of the Year in 2013.

Like many architects of his generation, Mikhail had accrued some capital working on and buying and selling little properties, so the architects didn't have to borrow the money to buy their first site. He observes that this was 'key, because it meant that we didn't have to pay interest right from the word go'.[8]

But he remembers the worry leading up to the auction: 'I'd done a couple of schemes the night before the auction and I was leaving the office late and I got mugged, so my bike and all my drawings got stolen. It was a pretty hideous experience. And I went to the auction thinking, "Is this a sign? Should I not be doing this?" Interestingly, I met a friend who said that he looked at the same site and decided he couldn't imagine how he would build anything there. Planning was the big anxiety.'

This was because, like many small inner-city sites, it was badly overlooked. Mikhail Riches' architectural solution not only overcame the many objections from neighbours, but it also increased the original gross internal area (GIA) of the planning permission the site was sold with by 60%.

Mikhail says the decision to take on a planning consultant was critical in helping them win planning. 'I never imagined for one second that we wouldn't get planning but the council was really on its knees financially at that point so dealing with them was very difficult ... the planning consultant just took over the whole process. She spoke their language and knew how to write emails that would get a response. She knew how to be incredibly polite and respectful in a way that I couldn't.'

The architects used a contractor who had worked for them on previous projects and managed to get a very good price from him, so the project became affordable. They also separated the groundworks – 'which tend to be very risky, so contractors tend to pile on a lot of risk money', Mikhail explains – and went out to a separate groundwork crew who built the foundations before doing the superstructure, which was just as well because they found an eighteenth-century well in the middle of the site.

Their other luck was timing because there had been a huge jump in London's property values from when the architects bought the site to almost six years later, when they finally secured planning permission and were ready to start the build. 'I was going to make so much more money than I could as an architect. It was ridiculous. Just by sitting on it and getting on with the day job rather than doing development I made money. I was in the right place at the right time. I don't think it's much to do with us if I'm honest. I think we're just lucky to be part of the "boomer" generation.'

Figure 4.16 Mikhail Riches, Church Walk, Hackney, London. The stepped volume creates balconies on each level and a series of gardens at the back of the building can be accessed from any of the ground-floor homes.

Figure 4.17 Mikhail Riches, Church Walk, Hackney, London. The architects wanted to prove they could work at a bigger scale having cut their teeth on house extensions. The development helped put the practice on the map.

Figure 4.18 (above) Mikhail Riches, Church Walk, Hackney, London. Over the years, the architects have lived in three of the properties, which has given them a unique insight into what works and what doesn't.

Figure 4.19 (below) Mikhail Riches, Church Walk, Hackney, London. The development comprises two houses and two apartments. The project is a detailed response to themes of density, overlooking and overshadowing that are common to small urban sites.

CHAPTER 5
FINDING FINANCE

The primary requirement for any development is of course finance. But how do you begin to raise the money that will help you to bring your imagined development opportunity into reality? There are three main avenues: your own cash, third-party equity and debt.

It's likely you will encounter at least two, if not three, of these options on your first project, so you'll need to be familiar with the terms, their advantages, disadvantages and the implications of each route. Remember: finance is the number one reason why people go bust and projects fail.

As our interviews make clear, there's a divide between the generation of architect developers who might not have started with cash in their pocket but went to university for free and were able to accrue money from flat conversions in the 1990s and early 2000s, and the subsequent generation. For the latter group things have been much harder, compounded now by higher interest rates and inflation.

It is hard to raise finance without a track record so be prepared to be patient. Arranging finance takes time, which can cause problems if you have bought a site at an auction and have just 20 working days to complete the purchase, as happened to Alex Wright (see later in this chapter), forcing him to use an expensive bridging loan to avoid losing his deposit. For Diana Borland and her business partner James Sanderson borrowing costs seriously affected their bottom line – but they had no choice (see chapter 2). Without cash you are at the mercy of lenders so make sure you understand the terms of the loan before you sign.

DEBT AND EQUITY

Debt is what you borrow. Whatever happens you will owe that money plus an interest payment. Equity is everything else. Normally, it's what you or your investors put into the project as cash. If you own your own home, your equity is what is left over when you subtract your outstanding mortgage from the value of the home. Equity can go up or down and can go to zero or can even go negative depending on the value of the asset and the amount of debt you have. Debt is fixed and can only go down if you pay it off. Leverage is the relationship between debt and equity and is calculated as debt divided by equity. For example, a house which is worth £500,000 on which you owe £300,000 to the bank has equity of £200,000. It has a Loan to Value of 60% (£300,000 divided by £500,000) and leverage is debt divided by equity = 150% or 1.5 times. A typical development would have a leverage of between four and eight times.

The debt and equity hierarchy (see figure 5.1) shows that the senior debt generally pays for most of the development and takes the first charge on the land. It's the safest money and has the lowest interest rate.

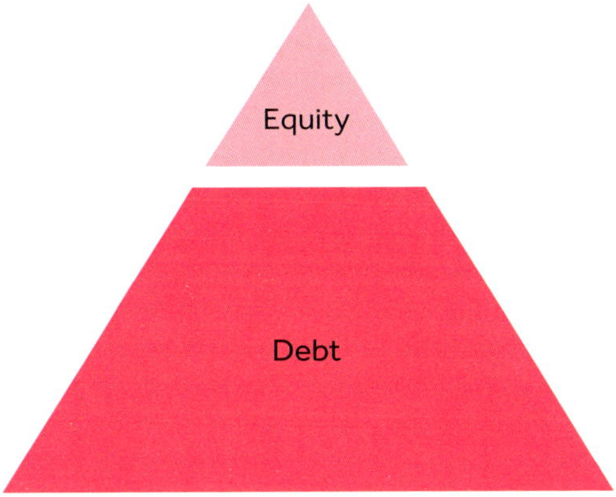

Figure 5.1 The debt and equity hierarchy.

DEBT

If you are not fortunate enough to be a 100% cash buyer, then you will need to explore some form of leverage to raise money as debt. This type of debt is often called 'vanilla debt' – bank debt, which is generally available from high street banks.

There are also 'challenger banks' and smaller lenders, who have a different risk appetite to the high street banks. All banks want the first charge on the land and you will need to have already obtained planning permission.[1]

The advantages of this kind of 'vanilla' or senior debt is that it's not your money. If it all goes wrong and the land is owned by a Special Purpose Vehicle (SPV), which we discuss in chapter 6, you can probably walk away with your shirt still on your back. However, the banks are wary of this and will try to tie you in in various ways, which will be explained later.

The other advantage of debt is that you can buy more than you can with cash. There are not many sites for sale at £100,000, but if you use that as equity and borrow £300,000, then you will find doors opening to many more sites. It will also give you a healthy return because you can use the power of leverage.

Using the numbers above you use your £100,000 in cash and your £300,000 loan to buy a house with potential to make into flats for £400,000, get planning permission for the flats and sell for £600,000. You owe the bank say 7%[2] of £300,000 x 1 year = £21,000 of interest costs plus the original £300,000. Your gross profit will be £179,000. On the other hand, if you buy a site in cash for £100,000 and get planning and sell for £150,000 you don't owe the bank anything, but your gross profit is just £50,000 which shows the potential power of leverage.

That said, to raise a loan you must have either a track record or a fantastic low-risk and high-return deal because banks see a lot of loan applications and will want to be sure of getting their money back.

All developers still need cash because the bank is not going to lend all the money and will want the developer to bear some of the risk. This is known as 'skin in the game'. How much will depend on the lender and how much the developer wants to borrow, and will involve 'debentures', effectively charges over a company. It's also likely that the developer could face a personal guarantee, which means if it all goes wrong they will personally promise to put their own money into the project. Of course these amounts can vary considerably, sometimes as much as 25% of the loan as a personal guarantee. It may seem like it could never happen to you, but try to avoid (or at least limit) personal guarantees if you possibly can.

Then there is the issue of who is going to pay for unforeseen costs if things do not go according to plan, and it will probably be you as the developer. Generally, the banks will be on the phone if you've budgeted for a £500,000 contract value and it's coming in at £600,000. It's likely they will want you to fund the extra £100,000 which is known as 'overspend'.

So, the timing of going to the bank is vital. If a developer goes too early without all the figures nailed down and a bunch of unfactored costs come in down the line, suddenly they will have to find more cash. Without deep pockets, the whole development is jeopardised, and can get taken back by the lender and sold to the highest bidder. In fact, there are some unscrupulous lenders out there who specifically use high-risk debt financing as a way to source sites.

SENIOR DEBT FINANCE

In relation to bank finance costs, there are generally two key ratios. The first ratio is the loan to cost ratio, effectively how much the entire project is going to cost and how much is borrowed.

It's safe to assume that banks will lend at a maximum of 80% loan to cost, but the devil is in the detail. In most instances you will have to include interest costs within your total cost, even though you haven't spent it yet. With some lenders you can put the value of the land in, while others only allow what you paid for it. If you paid for the land pre-planning and have added value, that means you aren't able to take advantage of the value uplift. It depends on each lender's attitude towards risk.

Example: *You buy a piece of land for £500,000 without planning permission. You then get planning permission and the value increases to £1,000,000. Total remaining costs are another £2,000,000 and you can borrow 80% of total costs. If you can borrow only on what you paid for the land then you can borrow 80% of £2,500,000, which is equal to £2,000,000. If you can borrow against the value of the land, you can borrow 80% of £3,000,000, which is £2,400,000.*

The second key ratio is loan to GDV (gross development value; see chapter 2), with the standard rate between 55% and 65%. The lower the rate the less risk there is for the lender, and the cheaper the interest rate. The ratio can also include the actual interest costs, so it is important to take care in working out the figures. Rates will be linked to the current Bank of England base rate and are normally variable rather than fixed.[3] Expect to pay in the region of 4–7% above the base rate. The big four clearing banks have the lowest appetite for risk and will normally lend at 65% loan to cost and 50% loan to value.

If you go to lenders outside the standard clearing banks, they'll lend more, they'll be more flexible and will be quicker than the high street banks, but they'll charge a significantly higher interest rate. You can in some instances borrow up to 95% of your costs.

One tip is to go back to the same lender once you've done a successful development with them. You will often find that with a track record with the same lender you'll get significantly more money at a lower cost.

We'd also recommend creating a good relationship with a broker, especially if you are just starting out. You will typically pay 1% of the lending amount to a broker but they are only paid on success. Good brokers know all of the lenders and what they like to lend on and they may be the difference between you getting the finance you need or not.

We've also noticed an increase in 'green' development funding. These are discounted loans which support more sustainable development projects. We suspect that this may be the sign of a new trend.

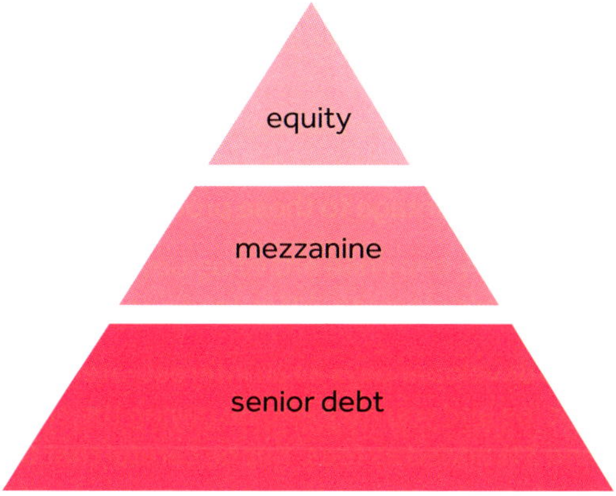

Figure 5.2 Mezzanine debt sits between debt and equity.

MEZZANINE DEBT

Now we move on from senior debt to mezzanine debt, which is generally accessed via brokers. In the risk hierarchy, it sits between senior debt and equity – senior at the bottom and equity at the top.

Mezzanine lenders generally take a second charge, which is a junior charge to the senior lender, and it means if anything goes wrong, the senior lender gets their money out before

If you now factor in that some of your cash came as equity, you'll quickly start to run into trouble. In the latter example, imagine that you have £100,000 in cash and raise £400,000 from investors at 10% interest rate per year. Now, you have the same rent at £40,000 but you have to pay the bank £25,000 and the investors £40,000, which doesn't stack up. In reality, the investors would have to take a lower return and share the £15,000, but your hard work and the £100,000 you invested will have come to nothing.

ANGEL INVESTORS

You may find a site that's £1,000,000 but you only have £50,000 in equity. You will almost certainly need to raise some kind of equity to complete the purchase.

Angel investors will put in somewhere between £20,000 and £100,000 each. However, they are unlikely to want to put £100,000 into a single project unless you have worked together before, or you have a great track record.

Unlike the start-up world, there are no easy places to find and pitch to angel investors in the property industry, so it's all about your network or finding someone with the network already in place.

Once you do find someone, they will want to know the extent of your 'skin in the game' – how much are you risking of your own money? Most investors will want to see you invest around 10% of the required equity. Investors will be looking at a 15– 20% IRR (internal rate of return; see chapter 2).

Typical structures

One way of setting up a deal is via a coupon plus a profit share. A coupon is another way of saying an interest payment. So you might say: I can offer a 10% coupon for the duration of the project and then I will share profit at the end. As an example, you raise £100,000 from the investor (as equity). You pay them £10,000 per year plus 25% of the profit. Alternatively, the investor might just prefer to do a profit share only and put in £100,000 for 50% of the profit.

Another version, which is also common, is called the 'waterfall method', where the investor gets the first 10% and if there's enough left over you get the next 10% as the developer. Then you share the rest 50/50.

FRIENDLY LOANS

Money can also be raised via 'friendly loans'. Many architect developers start out in this way with the help of friends and family.

The advantages are that it is almost certainly cheaper than going out to external investors and it should be simpler because if the money is coming from people you know, you won't necessarily have to convince them of your track record. More likely also is that your interests are going to be culturally aligned so it will hopefully allow you to get on with the project in the way that you want to – as long as the numbers stack up. You can sell friends and family an exciting vision with the promise of 10–15% a year interest rate, which for most people is very attractive.

The downside concerns legal requirements and set-up and making sure you don't fall foul of the Financial Conduct Authority, which regulates banks and investments, and particularly ensuring you are not inadvertently running a collective investment scheme, which without a licence is a criminal offence.

PEER-TO-PEER LENDING AND CROWDFUNDING

There has been a recent emergence of peer-to-peer lending (debt) or crowdfunding (equity) in the property industry. This effectively takes the concept of friendly family loans but brings in third-party strangers to back your project. You will generally pay an arrangement fee of 5% to these platforms. Crowd funders prefer a track record, but they are prepared to accept companies without if a strong case for the project can be made.

HOW TO GET A TRACK RECORD

You need to raise finance to do your first project, but you need to have done a project to raise the finance. Catch 22? Here are a few ideas.

Firstly, remember that a track record is about making the investors feel confident that you know what you are doing, that you're familiar with the language of the property industry and you have established contacts, even if you have not done a project yet yourself.

Entering into a joint venture (JV) with an existing developer is a good way architects without development experience can get started. Each party brings a skill set to the table so if you have an opportunity, and you pitch it to the right developer who shares your cultural interest and what you want to get out of it, then you both work on the project together and the developer raises the finance.

If you use cash you will not need to borrow anything so you could start with a smaller project. You could start with something that you are doing yourself, like a single house where you can go out and raise standard mortgage finance. Or you can use self-build mortgage finance, which gets you on the developer ladder because you can build that house, sell it on, use the equity, use the experience and then go and try to do the same with two houses instead of one. Or maybe you get together with a friend and you find a plot where you can build two houses, as Mark Shaw did, which we look at in more detail in chapter 7. The final approach is to try to convince your investors that you know what you're doing. If you have a good opportunity, you will always find money. Because if you can get an opportunity where the numbers stack up, and you are offering a 20% return, there will always be people interested.

A track record is really just a proxy for people to feel convinced that you know what you're doing. As we've said before, development is a rewarding but risky game and you need to convince your funding partners that they are not going to lose their money.

CASE STUDY

PROJECT	Sprowston Mews, London, UK
ARCHITECT DEVELOPER	Matheson Whiteley
COMPLETION	2020

After advising friends on development, both as architects and project managers, Donald Matheson and Jason Whiteley embarked on their own project – the redevelopment of an existing furniture-making workshop in Forest Gate, east London.

By the time they started to look for land in around 2016, values had crept up and demand was strong. They decided to team up with another couple who were friends of previous clients. Matheson explains, 'Their motivation was to get a working space and a home out of the deal. For us, it was about selling the units so we would be walking away from the project with a profit. By pooling resources, we knew we could buy the building for cash but the construction and project cost would have to be financed.'[7]

The financing of the project proved one of the hardest elements, says Matheson. It took them 12 months to find a lender. 'We had a couple of attempts to get finance from larger high street banks but without success and I was slightly at my wits' end about what to do. I was at a conference and one of the speakers talked specifically about finance.[8] I approached her afterwards and she became our broker and got us a deal with the United Trust Bank. She said to UTB, "These guys don't have any direct development experience with their own money, but they've been development managers on other projects."'

What ended up being the breakthrough was the bank's analysis of the architects' development appraisal, which showed a healthy 32% profit on cost return against a benchmark of 25%. Armed with this, the bank took the project to its development committee where it was approved.

The building was purchased through an SPV. Matheson explains, 'We set up a freehold company that owned the building comprising myself, my business partner Jason and the other couple, Max and Mariah. We were four equal directors in that company so we all had to give personal guarantees when we took the loan.'

He states, 'One advantage to the slight stop-start process with the finance was that we had time to get the project fairly well established in terms of planning and getting the contracts in place.' They tendered to four different contractors and ended up going with the lowest one because it best fitted with their development appraisal in terms of predicted construction costs.

As the development progressed, the architects were concerned about the quality of the work their contractor was delivering so they took over certain aspects of the build and managed them directly. Matheson says, 'It became almost like construction management, which obviously has a big cost in terms of time, but I don't regret doing that because we could introduce quality where we thought it would really matter.'

Figure 5.3 (above) Matheson Whiteley, Sprowston Mews, Forest Gate, London. The project redevelops an existing two-storey furniture-making workshop. Ground-floor workshops are retained and a new setback rooftop added.

Figure 5.4 (below) Matheson Whiteley, Sprowston Mews, Forest Gate, London. Kitchen space in one of the new apartments.

Figure 5.5 Matheson Whiteley, Sprowston Mews, Forest Gate, London. Any savings went into the design, for example the exposed ceiling joists in the timber-framed roof extension.

Further, he says, 'We tend to run things quite carefully in terms of contracts and I think with this particular project it was about drawing down on our loan gradually. I suppose that's another advantage architects have, which is as developers we can control that cash flow quite carefully to avoid paying unnecessary interest.'

The bank had been insistent on a 15% contingency, but as they didn't need to use it, they were able to spend it on exposed structural ceilings, which distinguished the flats in terms of design and helped boost the sales.

Matheson reflects, 'We were obsessive about keeping to our cost plan. I was often on site filling skips and digging holes for utilities companies so we'd be ready. There are certain things that make sense to take into your own hands, for example buying sanitary ware, tiles, flooring and appliances. We were quite relentless shopping around to get the best value and deliver against our development plan.'

Figure 5.6 Matheson Whiteley, Sprowston Mews, Forest Gate, London. A setback to the new roof extension forms south-facing external terraces.

Figure 5.7 Matheson Whiteley, Sprowston Mews, Forest Gate, London. The architects were concerned that the development's location, which contains light industrial business, would be a problem when it came to selling the apartments. In fact the opposite was true and they sold quickly.

Figure 5.8 Matheson Whiteley, Sprowston Mews, Forest Gate, London. Loggia terrace to the first-floor apartment.

CASE STUDY

PROJECT	Leybourne Road,London, UK
ARCHITECT DEVELOPER	Nelson Wright Architects
COMPLETION	2022

Architect Alex Wright and his partner Chelsea Nelson, an interior designer, bought their first site, a disused garage plot, in Leytonstone, east London in 2018. More recently they bought a second site in Peckham, south London.

The couple had not planned to become developers. Having lived locally in a rented house they wanted to build their own home and had spent many months scouring the area looking for sites, eventually finding one at auction.

'We bought the site with planning permission for one house on it and the intention initially was to just improve it. We saw that the current scheme, which had planning consent, was quite conservative and we thought we could do a bit of a better job for less money and make a better product,' says Wright.[9]

For the auction, they used their savings to put down a £25,000 deposit and used a bridging loan against Wright's mother's house for the outstanding £226,500. As with most auctions, they had only 20 working days to complete the finance.

Wright admits that he hadn't realised the time it would take to arrange the bridging loan, given the complex structure and the risk involved if they hadn't been able to complete all the paperwork in time. Not only would they have lost their deposit, they would also have been liable for the difference between the agreed price and the new sale price if the owner had needed to sell the site at a loss. The finance came through with just an hour to spare.

Figure 5.9 (opposite, above) Nelson Wright, Leybourne Road, London. The design is a contemporary interpretation of the existing terrace. Slender Belgian bricks and high-performance Danish windows create a blend of traditional and modern.

Figure 5.10 (opposite, below) Nelson Wright, Leybourne Road, London. Bespoke lights and furniture have been carefully designed for each space. Glass doors lead out to a walled garden.

80
82

Figure 5.11 (opposite) Nelson Wright, Leybourne Road, London. To create a sense of space, the architect has played with height and scale. The entrance hall is triple-height with a circular skylight reaching up to the pitched roof.

A few weeks after the site had been purchased, their neighbour offered to sell them an extra piece of land, roughly half the size of their existing site which, depending on planning, had the potential to change the scope of the project. They decided to make two applications, one for a revised house scheme and the other for two houses, in order to improve their negotiating position with the site's owner.

After successfully gaining planning permission for two houses, things became easier thanks to a healthy sales forecast for the second house. They had also struck a good deal with their neighbour, paying him half of what their site had cost based on it being half the size.

'The gross development value was reasonably high relative to the construction cost plus site costs, which helped arrange the finance and being qualified architects also helped,' Wright explains.

Following the successful application for two houses, the scope of the project increased, affecting the finance strategy slightly. The bridging loan was refinanced to a standard interest-only mortgage against the house, leaving the development site unencumbered and reducing the monthly payments. They also took advice from various specialists on the best way to split ownership of the two sites and decided, based on the advice, to set up a company, which also allowed them to borrow finance more easily as due to financial regulation development finance is harder to raise as individuals than as a business.

Wright says, 'We approached finance companies essentially with the proposal, "Look, we own this plot and we're going to buy this extra piece of land and this is how much extra money we need to buy the plot and then this is how much money we need to build and this is how we can pay it back." And actually, it was a lot more straightforward doing that than arranging the bridging loan.'

The house sold through The Modern House in just two weeks and they immediately began the search for a second site.

'We don't have the cash available to risk on a site without planning at the moment. If we did, it would be great because ultimately your margins are much higher, but architects who don't have huge amounts of capital available can make it work because they can add value. And I think as architects you have to just have a bit of belief in what you do. If we can do as good a job on the next project as we did on this I have every confidence that it will do quite well.'

Figure 5.12 Nelson Wright, Leybourne Road, London. All the rooms have sliding pocket doors to create semi-open-plan spaces on the ground floor.

CHAPTER 6
DOING THE DEAL

Now we come to how to make the deal happen. We'll be looking at the intricacies of the different ways to buy land and raise finance, and examine in detail the complexities of the different purchase contracts, option contracts, conditional or unconditional contracts, overage, private treaty, buying at auction, joint ventures with other parties and even how to buy land without any money.

We start with the two most common ways to buy land:

AUCTIONS

As we said in chapter 4, one of the simpler routes to buying land is via an auction. Land is often sold this way, particularly for smaller parcels that you will likely be looking to buy. It is a very short process. From the point at which an auction catalogue is released, you have about two to three weeks to do all of your due diligence, and that's why it is important to have the right team in place prior to starting your investigation. As a result of the extra risk you are taking on, land should theoretically be cheaper to buy at auction. However, auction fever can quickly take over, so make sure that if you go down this route you stick to your price and do not go over it.

The short time frame means that you must have your funding lined up; if you win the site in the auction you have to exchange on the site and put down 10% right away. If you don't have the funds available, you face being sued. Further, if you can't complete the purchase with the remaining 90% in the time frame allowed you will lose your deposit.

All bids are transparent. You know that you won't get gazumped if you make the highest bid. But beware, it's sometimes the person who understands the least or has done the least amount of due diligence who buys the site.

Our tip is to sign up to all the auction houses and look at the catalogues the day they are released. We would also encourage you to do a deal with your solicitor so that they will look over the legal pack for a fixed fee. You may also want them on standby on the day of the auction in case new information is released as it sometimes can be.

PRIVATE TREATY

Private treaty is also known as informal tender and is how the vast majority of land sales happen. When you buy a house through an estate agent it's through a private treaty: one buyer to one seller. One advantage of this route is that it gives you time because while something is on the market you can go out and raise funding and you can do your due diligence while lawyers are looking through and negotiating all the sales contracts. If you're very quick, you may even be able to put in a planning pre-application to get a sense of what you might be able to build before you commit to the purchase.

Timing is always an issue for the vendor because they will want to know when to expect their money. This only happens when you complete, so the agent will be desperately keen to know how long this will take. This is probably one of the reasons why vendors and agents are not always keen on selling anything other than an unconditional contract (discussed below) because in every other contract, they may have to wait a long time for their money.

Agents like to sell to developers who move quickly: the quicker you can move, the quicker they get their commission. Many developers will promise to complete within seven days but, in reality, this happens only rarely and where the developer is prepared to take quite a lot of risk. Even if agents demand a quick exchange and completion, it seldom happens that way.

The other advantage of a private treaty is that you can make a bespoke offer (discussed in detail below). It's worth making an offer that has several 'reasonable' conditions (for example, vacant possession), but expect the agent to push back via negotiation if the list is too long or unreasonable.

Finally, bear in mind that unlike in auction sales, you can be working on a transaction for a long time and at any point before exchange the contract can be taken away from you without any cost recovery. This gives unscrupulous agents the opportunity to let their friends know your bid and how to beat it.

We now talk about the several different contracts you can use when you are buying under private treaty.

OPTION CONTRACTS

Option contracts are a right but not an obligation to buy in the future. What this means is you can buy a piece of land for a fixed price, but you don't have to, so it's effectively an exclusivity agreement whereby the other party cannot sell to anybody else. It takes the land off the market and secures your position. And it means, if you find anything nasty or you don't succeed in getting planning, you can simply let the option expire and walk away.

You typically pay for an option, from as little as £1 to around 1–2% of the land price. This helps with your cash flow and reduces your risk as it allows you to have certainty before committing to the purchase. Although do note that the option may put obligations on you to perform to certain milestones, for example, putting in a planning application within a certain time, and note that you will have to pay for the costs to take the project to planning, which can add up to tens of thousands of pounds on a small development.

It is advisable with option contracts to negotiate up front a few things that may (and probably will) happen.

First if you have a 12-month option, try to negotiate the price for an extra six or 12 months. You don't want to find yourself held hostage by the landowner if you have spent tens of thousands of pounds and just need another few months to secure planning permission.

Second, it's worth negotiating a few other common 'what ifs':

- What if you get planning for less (or more) than you initially expected?
- What if costs are higher than you anticipated?
- What if the market has gone into freefall, or gone in your favour?

It's always best to do this up front as you're in a better negotiating position before you sign the option than when it's about to expire.

Option contracts can be legally simple or very complex. They can be a page long, but they can also be tens of pages long and take years to negotiate. This partly depends on your lawyers and partly depends on the lawyers of the landowner. Contracts are completed at the speed of the slowest lawyers. Don't be surprised if you are asked to contribute towards the costs of the landowner's legal fees, it's quite common. If you are paying, you may want to insist on the landowner using a lawyer you know can perform quickly.

The downside of options from a landowner's perspective is that they have to wait before they see any money. Generally, that's because as the developer you will need to have planning before exercising the option. Therefore, it can take time and be difficult to persuade landowners to give you an option. That's truer in cities where land is scarcer to come by and developers are willing to take the risk on planning. Bear in mind also that land sold via option will generally cost much more via an option than if it is purchased unconditionally.

CONDITIONAL CONTRACTS

Conditional contracts are pretty standard outside London or on larger plots of land. Most landowners outside of London recognise that planning is a major issue and they are not going to sell a site without having given you a chance to secure a planning consent and they don't normally expect you to put in all of your money up front. The normal way of dealing with these conditions is on what's called a 'subject to planning' (STP) basis. But note: it could be subject to other things as well. For example, it could be conditional on removing squatters, or getting vacant possession, or decontamination, and equally it could be conditional on sorting out a discrepancy on the Land Registry title or removing covenants. They all amount to the same thing: you only pay once that condition has been satisfied.

In a conditional contract, you commit to buying the land by exchanging contracts and paying a deposit. You would normally expect to pay a 10% deposit, although you could negotiate this down to 5%. The deposit sits in an escrow account with your or their solicitor, and then you complete (i.e. pay the balance of the money owed) within a set period of time once that conditionality becomes unconditional, for example, once you receive planning permission. Do not wait until you have planning before sourcing the finance. If you don't complete on the land, not only will you lose your deposit, your time and the money spent on the planning permission, the landowner will be given your deposit and their land will have the benefit of your planning. On the other hand, you should make sure that you have the option to complete with or without the conditionality being met. This protects your investment to a certain degree and gives you flexibility should you want to sell the land or change the planning permission to something else.

The advantage of conditional contracts is that they reduce your risk. If planning permission is not granted, then the contract is cancelled and you get your deposit back (unlike the option fee where it is paid up front and is non-refundable). It's better for your cash flow than buying the land unconditionally because you don't need to pay more than the legal costs of buying the land, the deposit and the cost of planning. Since you can't raise debt on land without planning, you reduce your reliance on expensive equity and can secure the permission and then raise cheaper debt finance. That's why it's a helpful mechanism for smaller developers or those without a huge amount of equity in their pockets. It's also easier to raise debt finance than equity finance.

The downside is that a conditional contract increases the risk for the seller as they are bound to you for a period.[1] They don't have a choice of going elsewhere and they don't have a chance to change their mind. As a result, the land will be generally more expensive than buying it unconditionally, although it will probably cost a bit less than if you had bought it by option.

Let's say you need to raise 10% for the deposit of a £2,000,000 site purchase, which is £200,000. If you don't have that much sitting in your back pocket you have to raise it from an investor, who you're paying 15–20% a year, which soon adds up. So you could try offering the landowner £2,100,000 with no deposit. This saves you from raising expensive equity and creates a win/win for you and the landowner. These are part of the negotiating tactics that you will need to have in your arsenal.

Conditional contracts can also be complicated because you have to think of the 'what ifs'. Being conditional on planning sounds relatively simple, but what happens if the planning that you get is not one you can implement? Or the planning you are given is for less than you wanted? If you have based your figures on a nine-unit scheme, but in the end the planning is only for a seven-unit scheme, how do you put that into the contract? These are some of the variables you have to consider in both the contract and when you're doing the deal with the landowner. As with an option, you should try to put as many what ifs into the contract as possible because it is easier to negotiate at the beginning than at the end.

UNCONDITIONAL CONTRACTS

Unconditional contracts are comparatively straightforward – you buy what you see. The only conditionality in an unconditional bid is generally the contract itself, or what's called 'subject to contract'. If you bid for land, always make sure you say 'subject to contract' in case the contract contains clauses which are unacceptable or may require you to change your offer. The only time you cannot change your offer is if you are bidding under auction conditions when it is expected that you have read and accepted the contract.

Unconditional contracts are attractive from a seller's perspective if they need money quickly. In a hot land market, the theoretical difference in price between conditional and unconditional contracts is reduced to an extent that it makes no sense for a landowner to wait around while you try to get planning permission.

As we've said before, unless you are a cash buyer, buying land without any planning is expensive because you have to raise equity from third-party investors who will want 15–20%

return per year. So, on your first project, you could do what many of the architect developers in the book have done and look for land that already has planning for something or an existing building, which you think you can enhance. For example, maybe it's land that has been granted planning for two houses and you think you can increase it by an adding a third house or maybe the permission is for a poor-quality scheme that you can improve. These are your unique skills and give you the competitive advantage over non-architects. If there is a building on the site or it has an existing planning permission, you can raise cheaper debt to buy the land and then try to enhance the planning to increase the value of that land and your profitability.

The downside to unconditional contracts is that you're taking all the risk on planning and you must really think carefully about your funding sources before you buy the land. Are you going to get your money from a high-net-worth individual? Can you do something clever with an existing planning permission where you can raise some debt? Bear in mind also that even if you are buying land unconditionally, it can still take a year or even two years to complete the deal, especially if you're dealing with a private landowner.

As mentioned above, sometimes it's possible to reduce your planning risk before you buy the land if you can act quickly. For example, you could potentially get some early pre-application advice from the planning authority while you're asking your lawyers to do the due diligence (and you can drag out purchases as long as you want, but beware that if you take too long the seller may pull their contract). The advantage of taking pre-application advice before you have committed is that by the time you enter into contract to buy the land, you and your investors will have got a good steer on the likely planning outcome. If you have a letter of support from the planners it will make raising money much easier, whereas if the planners have said 'no way' you can either use this as leverage to renegotiate the price with the landowner or pull out altogether.

DEFERRED UNCONDITIONAL

Deferred unconditional means that you are contracted to give the vendor a specific sum at a particular date in the future. The deferred timescale can be anything from six months to two years. This differs from a conditional contract, which states: 'We will give you £X if we get planning for five houses.'

The advantage of this contract is that it is more attractive to sellers than a conditional contract. They may have to wait a year, but they know that there's a lower risk of them not receiving the money. If you default, they keep your deposit of 5–10%. It is still good for your cash flow and, since the risk is lower to the seller, the land is going to be cheaper than if you buy land under a conditional contract. In terms of price and risk, it sits halfway between a conditional contract and an unconditional contract.

The downside of a deferred contract is that you are still committed to making the purchase even if you aren't successful in gaining planning permission. If you are hoping to get planning permission and raise the funding in the time you have deferred the sum and it doesn't work out, you will lose the deposit and all the time and money spent on planning. There is also a small chance that the seller might come after you for the rest of the money.

It can take a lot of time negotiating all these different issues and 'what if' scenarios so again, make sure you understand exactly what happens after the deferred time has expired. Can you claim for an extension of time due to matters outside of your control? Beware that the more negotiations you enter into, the more complicated the contract becomes and the longer it takes to get all parties to agree.

BUILDING LEASE

Some vendors, especially public landowners who have a duty of care to taxpayers, may insist on you entering into a building lease rather than a contract to buy. You may be familiar with a long lease on a flat and this is broadly the same. It gives the freeholder (in this case the public landowner) control over the land under certain circumstances. Most commonly, there will be obligations and restrictions on you as the developer based on time or delivery. Beware of building leases, they can be very tricky to raise funding on for small developers.

OVERAGE

Since property is a long game, the industry has come up with lots of ways to deal with 'what if' scenarios. The most common is overage. This gives the landowner a certain extra sum on the basis of some conditionality. Most commonly, it says that you will pay more money to the vendor if x, y or z happens. Typically, overage is calculated with respect to sales or planning. However, overage provisions have kept many lawyers in business because they are complicated to draft and can be complicated to implement. So, while overage is an attractive carrot to dangle in front of vendors, experience shows that it does add a layer of complexity (which equals more time and money to lawyers). Overage creates a mechanism that aims to be fair to all parties. Planning and development operate in a high-risk environment and so it is a good way to share some of the possible upsides (and downsides) with the landowner.

Overage agreements are good for your cash flow because you can base numbers on your conservative estimates and you don't have to pay more for the land up front. It can also be good for cash flow because you may pay overage out of sales, or you may pay overage only once you've been given planning permission and have raised your debt financing. The downside is that agreeing to it can take a huge amount of time and depending on the overage you agree to you may end up reducing your profit, which may make financing harder.

Sales overage

Sales overage could be based on your GDV (gross development value; see chapter 2) or sales value per square foot. GDV is the most accurate measure as it considers the overall scheme: the number of units, the amount of square footage and the £/ft^2 sales value. However, it can be difficult to calculate and you have to wait until the very end of the project before having all the information.

A typical example may be that the market value of the five houses of 1,000ft^2 you intend to build are worth £500,000 or £500 per ft^2. Your GDV is £2,500,000. The landowner may think that the market is going up, so you offer the landowner an extra 25% for every additional £1 per ft^2 you achieve on sales. This means that if you achieve an average £600 per ft^2, then the landowner would receive an overage payment of 25% x £100 x 5 x 1,000 = £125,000.

The reason why GDV is a better bet for the landowner is that you may be given planning for six houses instead of the original five. In the example above, if the houses' market value remained at £500 per ft^2 then the landowner would not get any overage. So instead, the landowner may want to structure a deal that gives him or her 25% of any extra over £2,500,000 GDV. This means that if planning for six is successful, but the market stays the same, the landowner still benefits. In this case the landowner will get 25% of 6 x 1,000 x 500 - £2,500,000 = £125,000.

You need to be aware of how overage can affect your profitability, if overage is based on sales and not costs. If we use the previous example and assume that your costs are £2,000,000 and house price inflation is running at 10% so that the houses are now worth £550,000 and the GDV is now £2,750,000, you will owe £62,500 to the landowner: £2,750,000 - £2,500,000 x 25% = £62,500.

However, if costs have also gone up by 10% and your costs are now £2,200,000 then your profitability has just dropped from £500,000 to £487,500. Alternatively, if we assume you are given planning for six houses, you will have sales of £3,000,000 and may have costs of £2,400,000 (assuming profit on sales of 20% like in our first example). However, your overage is £125,000 so your profitability goes from £500,000 for five houses to £475,000 for six houses.

In order that you are protected in case sales receipts are less than you anticipated, you may be able to agree to a downward overage reduction as well as an upward overage payment. This may be unpalatable to landowners, so instead you could try to agree to a lower GDV baseline to protect yourself from overpaying in a falling market. In summary, if you have an agreement to pay overage based on sales make sure that you don't promise too much, keep your appraisal up to date and keep track of your profitability.

PLANNING OVERAGE

Basing your overage on planning is generally simpler and quicker and carries less risk to your profitability. In our example, you may simply pay an extra £50,000 for each extra house you are given planning for, or you could offer an extra £50 per ft^2 for any planning permission greater than 5,000ft^2. For example, planning has been granted for five 1,500ft^2 houses rather than 1,000ft^2. That means you get an extra 2,500ft^2 and pay £125,000. Generally, unless it triggers some other payment, the greater the amount of area you get planning permission for the greater the profitability. In planning overage, if you succeed in increasing the number of units and are prepared to pay more as a result, you should try to share some of the downside risk of planning too (i.e. you pay less if you get planning for fewer units).

BUYING LAND WITHOUT ANY MONEY

As a first-time developer, you will not have amassed much cash (equity) and so here are a few tips to get you started on how to buy land without any (or much) money.

JOINT VENTURE (JV) WITH A DEVELOPER

First of all you can do this through a joint venture with a property developer. If you are a designer or an architect, you can use your time in lieu of cash. For example, you invest the fees that you would normally charge as equity. You may offer to do all the design and planning work for free in return for a percentage of the project. The way to structure this is to look at your time investment as an equity investment. For example, if you would normally charge 5% on a £2,000,000 construction value project then that's the equivalent of £100,000. If the total costs are £3,000,000 and the equity requirement for the project is 20% (on an 80% loan to cost funding package), then equity required would be £600,000. That means your £100,000 sweat equity is worth ⅙ of the project and ⅙ of the profit. At the end of the project, if all goes to plan, you would expect to get your £100,000 in fees + ⅙ of the profit (approximately another £100,000).

If this sounds appealing, then network with developers who are earlier in their career and looking to cut their costs and share the rewards. Or better yet, if you've sourced an opportunity of your own that you can bring to a developer then you are in control and you can set the terms of the agreement.

The advantage to this method is that you need less money up front. It means you need less cash flow throughout the project and it can be an attractive proposition to a developer who will know that you are going to be working to get the best possible building at the best price and value.

You don't need to be an architect to do this – you could be a builder or another property professional, or even another developer and still strike up a JV. The same point applies: if you find the site, you control the situation. The downside to a JV is that you have got to make sure you find the right partner. It's easy to find someone who sounds great initially, but when you delve a bit deeper you may realise you have actually ended up with someone who doesn't share your values or your objectives. You must also think about what happens if things go wrong. It's important when you go into a business relationship with anyone to think through the 'what if' scenarios and this is where a lawyer will help you. At the minimum, you should have a plan for what happens if there is a disagreement, a stalemate, a lack of funding, or if something unforeseen happens to one or other of you.

JOINT VENTURE WITH LANDOWNERS

Joint ventures with landowners are a very common approach for developers. The landowner effectively contributes to the JV by putting the land in and you do everything else. A standard approach is via a promoter agreement, which is a business in and of itself. It works like this: you pay for and take the risk of securing planning on the land. The value of the land post-planning is then shared between you and the landowner. A typical promotion agreement will give 10–20% to the developer and 80–90% to the landowner after any hard costs. It is also possible to lock in a 'right to buy' for you as the promoter. The advantage to this is that it means you don't have to agree on a price on the land at the beginning of the deal and you don't have to buy the land up front.

For example, you enter into a promoter agreement for a 20/80 split. You pay £100,000 to take the land through planning and the land is then sold for £1,100,000 post-planning. You will get back your £100,000 leaving £1,000,000 to be split 20/80 in favour of the landowner. In this case you get another £200,000 with the landowner receiving the remaining £800,000. Promoter agreements are common when planning permission for a piece of land is likely to take time and money and the landowner doesn't want to take that risk or go through the effort. They are rare in cities but common on rural land.

The main advantage of this route is less money is needed up front, although you still have to commit to paying the planning costs and all other design fees; this is where you can use your skill set and your fees as equity. Another advantage is that you don't have to agree on a sale value up front. It can be an attractive proposition to a landowner as it's fairly straightforward and everyone is aligned to get the best planning permission for the site.

The downside to this approach is that it tends to be used on more difficult sites, which can take many years to get planning on. If you are interested in developing then you will want to negotiate up front the right to buy the land on planning for a specific price. By that time, you will have built up enough equity in the scheme to be able to draw down on debt to cover the development finance. You may also be able to convince the landowner to continue as a partner (although there are tax implications for this, so do talk to an advisor about how you structure this).

A typical route in cities is to do a JV with building owners for rooftop development. This is becoming more and more popular due to recent changes in planning legislation, making it easier to get planning for these types of development.[2] It generally works with blocks of flats. It tends to work well when work is needed on a roof and a deal can be done whereby you repair/replace the roof in return for building between flats in the airspace above the block. Things to be aware of are the engineering costs, building control and the legal implications in the leases of the various flat-owners and what they can and cannot do.

JOINT VENTURE WITH CUSTOMERS

Joint ventures with customers are unusual in the UK but more common in other countries. In Germany it's known as *baugruppen*, in Argentina it's called *fideicomiso*. In the UK, it can be known as 'co-housing', or 'group custom build' or 'group self-build'. There are lots of names for this, but effectively this is a group of customers who are going to buy a parcel of land and you are going to run the process for them. You won't necessarily get a share of the profit because there may not be a profit per se. Instead, you'll take a fee for managing the project. You will still effectively be a developer, because you're taking a bit of land and you're responsible for making sure it is built. It is similar, but not exactly the same, as development management, which more accurately describes your role if you are acting for a landowner (mainly investors) on a commercial basis than when you are acting for the occupiers themselves. Advantages of this route are that you're not having to put any money up front as the customers will finance the development, either from their own mortgage, which is typically cheaper than commercial debt, or from grants from a local authority or government. If you have successfully managed and completed the development this will help you convince a bank or investor to put money into the next opportunity as you will have gained the all-important 'track record'.

The downside is that you are dealing with lots of clients. You've got to find them (or they have to find you), you've got to manage them and create a common consensus working with group dynamics. And finally, you've got to work out who is taking the risk: is it you or is it them? This is all down to the structures, but something to consider.

JOINT VENTURE WITH SUPPLIERS

This is common in other industries but less common in development. However, it was used successfully recently at the Marmalade Lane project in Cambridge (developed by Town and designed by Mole Architects). In that case, the developer teamed up with a timber frame manufacturer from Sweden and ran the project for them while the timber frame manufacturer put all the funding in place and of course was also able to supply their timber frame.

The advantages here are that you can negotiate to be paid a management fee and you will get a bonus/profit share. The downside is that there aren't many suppliers that are willing to fund you and take development risk. You've still got to find the opportunity, and you're then tied into that supplier and their system. So it has got to be a manufacturer or a supplier that you like and one you want to use.

DEVELOPMENT MANAGER WITH INVESTORS

This is the most common way to get started in development. It means you are fully (or partially) investor backed. There are three things you need to agree with your investors. How much each party puts into the deal, how you split the profit and when everyone gets paid. With the right opportunity that shows the right levels of return, you can find investors that will back you 100% and you will not have to put any money in. The better the opportunity, the more likely the investors will overlook your lack of track record and your absence of funds.

However, this is dependent on finding great opportunities and being able to communicate it well with good third-party evidence. You should also try to find investors who share your values and your vision. If the investors are not aligned with what you want to build, you will end up working in a way and on a job that fails to sit well with you. Since developments can take many years, you should make sure you are working with people you like and on a project you find exciting and interesting.

STRUCTURING THE PURCHASE

SPECIAL PURPOSE VEHICLE (SPV)

The vast majority of land purchases are done using an SPV. This is a specially set up limited liability company that has one asset: the land or site.

The reasons for using an SPV are normally to reduce the potential liability if things go wrong. If the company goes bankrupt, then the owners of the company may lose the money they invested but won't lose any of their personal assets. It's also easy to shut down a company once all the properties are sold and money distributed.

SPVs can be advantageous from a tax perspective. For example, you may find that you need to sell the land. In the case of an SPV, another company can buy the SPV rather than the land, saving thousands of pounds in stamp duty.

Companies can also be VAT registered allowing you to save money on professional fees. VAT is a complex subject, but the general principle is that change of use and new-build get special VAT treatments, so you should seek specialist advice on this before you structure the company.

OTHER LEGAL STRUCTURES

Apart from SPVs, you may want to consider limited liability partnerships or trusts. Communities may also want to look at Community Interest Companies (CIC) or Community Land Trusts.

CASE STUDY

PROJECT	Bath Street, Edinburgh, UK
ARCHITECT DEVELOPER	John Kinsley Architects
COMPLETION	2017

Architect John Kinsley's pioneering co-housing project in Portobello, Edinburgh, was inspired by the *baugruppen* model of development, a form of self-organised collective housing, or co-housing, that flourishes in Europe. In Berlin one in ten new homes are procured in this way.

Co-housing, also known as community-led housing, is still a relatively new concept in the UK and has been slow to take off mainly because of the cost of land especially in cities like London and Edinburgh.

Kinsley's client for Bath Street, Portobello was a group of four families (of which he was one) who Kinsley found via a community website. They formed a company to purchase the site and built a small tenement block.

For architects looking for an alternative path to being in a developer role, co-housing has much to recommend it. First, it's a way to help ease some of the problems of the housing market. Second, it fosters a sense of community by bringing together like-minded people inspired by the idea of a bespoke home – in this case, with exemplary environmental credentials. And perhaps most importantly of all, the developer's profit is removed from the equation, allowing each house to be purchased at cost.

For Kinsley, as the architect and facilitator, the process is also more rewarding than working for a traditional developer. As he explains, 'It puts the architect more centrally within the process … Rather than working with a developer who is inclined to bang you over the head every so often and tell you, "No, you can't do that," working with end-user participant clients is more creative because they've bought into this kind of fairly unusual process.'[3]

Kinsley was lucky that the landowner was someone he knew and was agreeable to a handshake deal subject to planning approval, giving him time to put the group together before having to write the cheque.

As the architect, he funded the project up to the outline design stage (RIBA Stage 2) with enough detail to complete a development appraisal and give participants an idea of what the scheme would look like, its overall size and what a typical unit size might be. This was enough for the other parties to be able to commit to the project and put money into it so they could buy the land with cash.

Figure 6.1 (above) John Kinsley Architects, Bath Street, Edinburgh. View of the top-floor flat kitchen from the living room.

Figure 6.2 (below) John Kinsley Architects, Bath Street, Edinburgh. The scheme is designed to Passivhaus equivalent levels of energy use.

Figure 6.3 John Kinsley Architects, Bath Street, Edinburgh. The new building is carefully integrated into the street by stepping the facade in both section and plan to address the change in scale from the Victorian tenement on one side and a Georgian house on the other.

Figure 6.4 (opposite) John Kinsley Architects, Bath Street, Edinburgh. A contextual approach also informs the selection of materials, with the main facade being predominantly red sandstone.

Figure 6.5 (above) John Kinsley Architects, Bath Street, Edinburgh. Bedroom of the top-floor flat.

Kinsley explains, 'We worked with the Ecology Building Society and they were pretty understanding compared to most kinds of conventional high-street lenders. They liked the model and the fact we were building to pretty high standards in terms of sustainability, and they were comfortable with the level of risk that was involved.'

They built to a kind of shell and core, which was paid to the contractors on a pro rata by floor area basis, while kitchen fit-outs, bathroom fit-outs and finishes were procured directly by the participants. They ring-fenced the costs on those so they could be allocated directly to the flat. Kinsley says, 'We had a good main contractor who was pretty flexible and was willing to allow quite a large degree of client fit-out as well.'

Figure 6.6 John Kinsley Architects, Bath Street, Edinburgh. The architect ran an 'open book' with the main contractor to allow it to fine tune building packages as they were about to be let in order to keep within the overall budget.

Figure 6.7 John Kinsley Architects, Bath Street, Edinburgh. The site during construction.

Further, he explains, 'We had a 5% contingency because money was tight, but we did deliver with that. We were running an "open book" with a main contractor, which meant whenever we were about to let a building package, we could fine tune it and do a little bit of value engineering on a package-by-package basis as we went along.'

Kinsley even tendered it to a different subcontractor in one or two cases as well, just to keep within the overall budget. Having a good, flexible main contractor helped with this process. On practical completion, ownership was transferred to the participants, who then resigned as directors from the company and the company was dissolved.

Kinsley is currently working on a number of other co-housing projects in Scotland including one in Leith. 'At the Leith site it has been a broadly similar process in that it's a private owner who's interested in the model and isn't necessarily wanting to just sell it quickly to the highest bidder. They're happy to give us a bit of time to put the group together because they like the social and environmental aspects of the model.'

CASE STUDY

PROJECT	Godson Street, London, UK
ARCHITECT DEVELOPER	Edgley Design and Spaced Out Architecture
COMPLETION	2015

Jake Edgley runs Edgley Design, a small practice in Southwark, central London, and has been developing since 2004 when he bought his first site in Islington, north London.

The five-person practice specialises in one-off private houses, work Edgley describes as immensely satisfying, but not profitable enough to sustain the office on its own. Development continues to be a way of increasing the practice's profitability without having to take on more staff.

'The whole challenge of developing is finding land, everything else is fairly easy and fairly fun. If you buy badly, you've absolutely had it. And if you buy well, you're probably okay,' Edgley says.[4]

Although most of his developments have been in north London, more recently he bought a shop with a flat above in Denmark Hill, south east London. He explains, 'We spent a year doing up the flat and the shop, but we didn't make any money from the sale. It was all about getting hold of the land at the back.'

Edgley notes that the internet has made it easier to research potential sites, but it also means it's easier for everyone else. 'When I look through the sites that I have ended up buying, they're nearly all off-market and come through an agent who I've been pestering for months.'

But as he is at pains to point out, they are not just ordinary high-street agents, but slightly shadowy figures who probably don't have an office or address because they don't want to be pestered. 'When you approach them, it's important to understand you're selling yourself. You're not going to them and saying, "Show me what you've got," you're saying, "Please, can you offer me a piece of land and I won't let you down?"'

To help the process along, Edgley always provides the agent with his track record, including how he's raised the finance and the planning permissions he has managed to achieve on difficult sites and any other information that demonstrates experience. 'These are often very small deals for the agents, so the fees are small and the sites are tricky to sell and often the agents are only co-operating because they want the resales at the end of the development, which you have to do if you want to keep them on side,' says Edgley.

He concludes, 'When you're looking for sites, you have to have a really open mind. It gets harder when you've been doing it for a while because you end up looking for something you've done before, when actually the next opportunity might be very different.'

Figure 6.8 Edgley Design, CKS Partnership and Spaced Out Architecture, Godson Street, London. A development of five mixed-use buildings containing commercial space on the ground and basement levels with residential apartments above and a townhouse to the north.

Figure 6.9 (opposite) Edgley Design, CKS Partnership and Spaced Out Architecture, Godson Street, London. The three partners were all neighbours of the vacant site and formed a JV partnership to buy and develop the scheme.

Figure 6.10 (above) Edgley Design, CKS Partnership and Spaced Out Architecture, Godson Street, London. A lightweight timber stud and glue-laminated framework was used for the residential part of the development so that alterations could be made on site during construction.

Figure 6.11 (above) Edgley Design, CKS Partnership and Spaced Out Architecture, Godson Street, London. Edgley Design moved into one of the commercial premises at Godson Street.

Figure 6.12 (below) Edgley Design, CKS Partnership and Spaced Out Architecture, Godson Street, London. The stepped roof shape was designed so as not to block light for neighbouring properties.

CASE STUDY

PROJECT	Tobacco Factory, Bristol, UK
ARCHITECT DEVELOPER	George Ferguson
COMPLETION	2001

Previously known as the Franklyn Davey & Co. building, the Tobacco Factory was built in 1912 to the design of Sir Frank Wills, the architect of many Bristol landmarks and institutions. In 1993 the majority of the Imperial Tobacco buildings were being demolished but architect George Ferguson bought a key one to save it for creative re-use.

The 4,000 sqm Tobacco Factory now houses a large cafe/bar, farm shop, local market, creative industry workspace, as well as the Tobacco Factory Theatre and Bristol School of Acting.

Ferguson did not set out to become a developer. His first involvement was to try to save the complex from demolition by persuading a developer to buy it with Ferguson's practice acting as the architect. But the developer lost his nerve and sold the buildings which eventually ended up in the hands of the receiver who advised that the site should be cleared. In desperation, Ferguson made one last-ditch attempt and offered to buy the corner building. 'It was on the market for £400,000 so I asked the demolition guy his quote to knock it down, which was £250,000 so I said (to the receiver), "I'll save you the demolition costs and give you £185,000," and they said, "Make it £200,000 and you can have it." I sweated then because I didn't have the money and I didn't really have a plan but I knew I could do something with it.'[5]

It took Ferguson seven years to make the building work as a thriving mixed-use development. 'I was very much ripping off what Ernest Hall had done in Halifax. It was a leap in the dark, but I knew it was an opportunity to do all those things that I'd always wanted to do for clients. But I also knew that any client who bought a building like this would either turn it into flats or offices. They wouldn't mix it up. So, my reason for going into development was to demonstrate that you can make things complicated and still make them work.'[6]

Banks wouldn't lend to him so he had to borrow money from family and friends – but this gave him the freedom to develop his vision as he went along, a luxury few first-time developers ever have. His principle was that 25% of the building would be cultural because he knew the rest of the building would become more valuable as a result of the theatre and the other arts uses. His first income came from renting existing office space in the building.

Figure 6.13 (above) Ferguson Mann, Tobacco Factory, Southville, Bristol. Ferguson set about creating different enterprises, such as weekly markets, to make the place interesting and add value.

Figure 6.14 (below) Ferguson Mann, Tobacco Factory, Southville, Bristol. From the outset, offices produced an income but now a significant proportion of the workspace is for creative industry and educational.

Figure 6.15 Ferguson Mann, Tobacco Factory, Southville, Bristol. The theatre created value by becoming a cultural attraction and was initially given to a theatre group rent free.

'I thought the easiest thing was just to paint the offices, scrub the floors and install some heating system so that started the whole thing rolling and after the second year I had a guaranteed income.'

To ensure he had the right mix of tenants, he gave three-year leases with a three-month notice period (except for the theatre, which has a 999-year lease). 'I was always able to adjust things and in a thriving, mixed-use building it's important not to lock yourself in with people who might change. And they do change so make quite sure you've got bombproof leases and you write your principles into the leases.'

Ferguson, who remains involved in the Tobacco Factory and related businesses, including a bakery and farm, says that despite its huge success, the Tobacco Factory was never a property project. 'It was a creative project about creating lots of different enterprises that make the place interesting. But of course you add value as you're going along.'

Figure 6.16 Ferguson Mann, Tobacco Factory, Southville, Bristol. Inspired by the lofts he had seen in Manhattan, Ferguson converted the top floor of the building into seven live/work apartments where he also lived for 18 years.

CHAPTER 7
HOW TO MANAGE YOUR PROJECT

In this chapter we will explore how best to manage and deliver your project. Working with builders can be fraught, often leading to legal disputes, but it's another area where architects have a lot of prior experience and contacts, both of which are essential for successful development.

If you have made the decision to become a developer, the likelihood is you enjoy, or thought you enjoyed, construction. And maybe you feel a sense of frustration that your role as an architect has become separated from actual *building* and part of you is relishing the chance to be more involved in the construction process.

Many of the architects we spoke to have had direct experience of construction from doing individual houses or house renovations. What this has taught them is that the best way to manage the process is to be highly organised and think ahead about how you are going to build your development with the budget you have.

Carl Turner, architect developer of the successful Pop Brixton project (see later in this chapter), enjoys the challenge. He says having to find solutions quickly and adapting the design to the budget is 'a bit more like working as a sculptor. When you're on site you're just dealing with things and shaping them and in some respects I didn't know what I didn't know, so, there wasn't a fear factor.'[1]

Other architect developers have commented on how the experience has made them more aware of the cost implications of their designs. Looking back, some have admitted that they could have delivered a simpler scheme with the same amount of space, and it would not have cost as much to build. David Miklhail says, 'It's important that you appreciate the amount of energy and effort that goes into making a building, so you don't just draw shit lightly.'[2] A truer word was never spoken!

THE PROJECT TRIANGLE

Before starting any project, you will need to decide what you want to prioritise and what are you are prepared to compromise on in the project triangle.

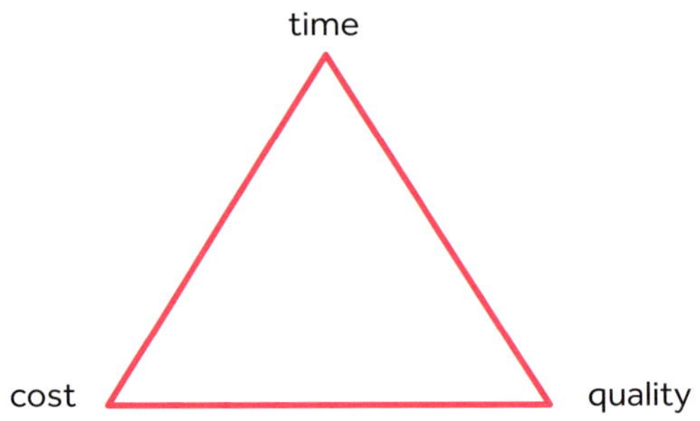

Figure 7.1 Project triangle

The project triangle is almost a law for all projects large or small. It has three outcomes, which are the essential decisions of any project. They are: time, cost and quality.

BEST CONSTRUCTION ROUTE

The rule is that your project can succeed on any two outcomes but not all three. You can have a high-quality project that is quick, but it won't be cheap. You can bring your project in on budget with the right level of quality, but it will take a long time to complete. Or you can deliver a cheap and quick project, but the quality of the project will suffer.

As an architect, it's unlikely you will want to compromise on quality, so you need to decide whether you are prepared for the project to cost more or take longer. You will hear people who say they have managed to achieve all three, but this is typically only achievable if your budget is high, there is a low quality expectation and you have a lot of time on your hands. For most projects, that doesn't apply; as a developer, you are stuck between a rock and a hard place. Your funders will want the project completed quickly, customers will demand a high-quality project and you will want to keep costs down to make sure you make a profit.

Once you have decided where the project sits in the time-cost-quality triangle, you can then make some decisions around the construction and delivery of the project and the route you go down.

MAIN DIFFERENCES BETWEEN THE CONTRACT ROUTES

You can buy contracts off the shelf using the main providers who are the Joint Contracts Tribunal (normally known as a JCT contract and considered the standard) or the New Engineering Contract (NEC), which has been around for 30 years and is gaining in popularity, or you can go to a lawyer to get a bespoke contract. Bear in mind that the more bespoke a contract, or the more changes you make to an off-the-shelf contract, the more a contractor may want to bring in their lawyers or be turned off completely from the job.

Whichever provider you use, you will probably want to consider one of the three most common contractual routes we explore below:

Design and build (D&B) – priority: time and costs

Typically, design and build (D&B) is considered the best contract route if you want to fix your costs and time. In theory, you are passing the risk of the project over to the contractor, who will be contractually obligated to deliver to an agreed cost and timescale. In theory, you can leave them to it and come back when they've finished. Although we wouldn't advise managing your project that way!

With certain exceptions, they will be responsible for everything, including most of the unforeseen risk. However, they will have flexibility in terms of the design, the way they build and some of the materials they use. This often creates a lower quality building than other routes as contractors will be incentivised to cut costs where they can and you may not be happy with those decisions. Costs are guaranteed with a fixed-price contract and liquidated and ascertained damages (LADs) create a significant penalty if a contractor is late in delivery. But if you change your mind during the project, you will be hit with heavy penalties by the contractor so make sure you stay disciplined and do all your designing before you go to tender.

You can mitigate against a lower quality building by providing more drawings and more information up front. However, there is a balance, because the more you produce, the less likely it will be an attractive proposition for a D&B contractor, and you won't get attractive tender prices back.

Traditional – priority: time and quality

The main alternative to a D&B route is to use a traditional contract, which broadly sets out a contract to deliver the building in line with the contract documents but doesn't completely pass over all the risk of any unknown factors. Traditional contracts also have LADs and fixed prices, but these will be fought over as there are many allowable reasons for delays. If something unforeseen arises, you will be responsible for the extra cost or time. However, these contracts are more flexible in terms of changing the design or specification of the project which gives you more control over the quality.

Construction management or management contracting – priority: quality and costs

In construction management (CM), you employ a person, firm or contractor to act as your on-site project manager. You then enter a contract with all of the subcontract packages directly, but the contract manager will be responsible for getting quotes and presenting them to you for your approval.

In management contracting (MC) it is a similar arrangement, but the subcontract packages work under the management contractor who is paid a fee by you.

In both the above routes, prices and timescales are estimated but not fixed at the beginning of the project so you are liable for any cost (and time) increases. Many smaller developers will start out being the CM/MC themselves. This will entirely depend on your level of confidence and time you have available; it gives you the most amount of flexibility, but you take on the greatest risk.

CAVEATS

It should be noted that all of the routes come with potential risks, and none will completely protect you from either losing money, the project running over time or the quality being compromised. If your contractor is tightly bound up in a D&B contract and something happens, or they finish the project late, then you may have to resort to legal means to get your money back. This is an expensive and time-consuming route and often contractors will not be financially sound enough to make it worthwhile spending money to win what may become a pyrrhic victory. If a contractor does not have a strong balance sheet, no matter how much they are at fault, you will still stand to lose some, most or all of your money. It is therefore very important to check the financial standing of your contractor before you tender with them.

HOW MUCH DETAIL DO YOU PUT INTO A TENDER PACKAGE?

Depending on which contractual route you go down, you want to think about what goes into the tender pack. Too much and you risk it taking a long time to organise and overwhelming contractors. Too little and you risk a contractor having a lot of wriggle room when things don't go according to plan.

If you are going down a D&B route, you should consider specifying and drawing everything that is important to you in terms of the quality that you want to achieve. If you are going down a traditional or CM/MC route, then you will have more flexibility as you can design packages later down the line and once some of the building has been built.

HOW DO YOU PICK GOOD CONTRACTORS?

Picking a good contractor is essential to delivery. Three references are the obvious starting point and, ideally, you can find an independent review/reference for the contractor (not just people they direct you to). It's always worth seeing at least two to three of their recent jobs – maybe one in progress and one complete to see the standards of their finishing and whether they understand design. When you are on their site, observe how clean and tidy the site and the site office is, what the workers are doing and whether they and their subcontractors observe health and safety rules.

In terms of the size of contractor you should select, a good rule of thumb is to pick a contractor whose annual turnover is between six and seven times the cost of your project. Alternatively, your project should be one of five or six that the contractor is running. If it's a tiny project and a tiny percentage of turnover then you may not get enough attention from management, or they may not be interested in tendering. If it's a very large percentage of turnover, you may be in danger of making them too reliant on you and your project, which may put them into financial instability should anything not go according to plan.

WHAT DO YOU DO IF YOUR BUILDER GOES BUST?

If your builder goes bankrupt, the first thing is not to panic. It's not good news, but it is not always a disaster either. Contractors often work on thin margins, which means that, if a client is late in paying, or if they have mispriced a job, they are vulnerable to going bankrupt. This is one of the reasons you want to have all the building regulations and warranty paperwork in place. Asking the building inspector to sign off on a partially completed job is a headache and to be avoided if possible. You will need this and a warranty if you want to sell the development as they are generally a condition of any sale.

When the contractor goes bust the key is to decide whether you like the contractor and what they have done for you, or whether they have been difficult or slow. If you like the contractor and they have gone bust because a client has paid them late or something has happened that you feel was not necessarily their fault, you may encourage them to simply set up under a new name and finish your job under a new contract. If you don't like the contractor, then use this as an opportunity to find someone else to finish the job, but don't underestimate how problematic it can be, especially if subcontractors haven't been paid (which is highly likely when a main contractor goes bust).

In theory, you are somewhat protected if you have been doing valuations in arrears as the valuation process goes like this:

Days 1–30: builder does some work, pays for materials and labour
Day 30: valuation of the work is undertaken (generally by a quantity surveyor or contract administrator)
Days 30–45: valuation is agreed between all parties
Day 46: builder issues an invoice
Day 60: client pays invoice minus a 5% 'retention'
Day 60: valuation of days 31–60 is undertaken and the cycle repeats.

The theory is that you as the client are protected because a) you are only paying for work that has been done and b) the builder has in fact done even more work during days 30–60, which hasn't yet been paid for.

However, the reality with smaller contractors is that they will often delay payment to their subcontractors until they get paid and will have materials coming to the site on account or credit. So, while it may appear as if they have paid for materials up front, in fact they haven't necessarily done so and are in fact operating without much cash flow buffer. When contractors go bust, even though you may have kept up your payments to them, it doesn't mean that everyone who has worked on site will also have been paid. Ideally you want to make sure that your subcontractors are being paid so that, in the event of your main contractor going bust, they aren't left out of pocket, which may make finishing the job harder. One way to do this is to ask for proof of payment to subcontractors. Main contractors may be reluctant to do this, but it will help to protect you in the event of things going wrong.

The other thing to note about valuations is that sometimes what is left in the budget for a particular item does not actually cover the cost of getting that remaining item delivered by a new contractor. For example, if you have a plumbing price from your main contractor of £20,000 and they've completed say 50% of the work, it should cost £10,000 to finish the job. If they leave halfway through, however, and you are able to convince a new plumber to take over (not an easy task), you will likely have to pay a premium to the new plumber who may, for example, charge £12,000 to finish the job, leaving you £2,000 out of pocket. If your contractor goes bust it is therefore worth talking to their subcontractors to see if they want to work for you directly and finish what they started. Even if you have to pay more than you had in the budget, it may still be cheaper and will certainly be less of a headache than finding someone new and starting again.

WHAT TO DO ON A DAILY / WEEKLY / MONTHLY / QUARTERLY / ANNUAL BASIS

Once you have picked your contractor and signed the contract, your job will be to monitor the situation and deal closely with the contractor or your quantity surveyor to ensure timely delivery.

Firstly and most importantly take plenty of photographs and notes and make sure they are well documented. A 360-degree camera is relatively cheap these days and is an excellent way to record progress of a site over time.

The size of the job will dictate what frequency you should visit, but either you or one of your team should be going to site between once a week and once every two weeks, on average. At certain times of the project, for example during the groundworks stage, it may be possible to reduce this frequency. However, it is essential that someone is documenting what is going on in case any future problems arise. Overall, the more you can visit a site the better, and this is one of the reasons that building locally to where you live makes a lot of sense.

Ideally you will use software to create and monitor your programme as well as a Gantt chart. However, a spreadsheet with tasks can be just as effective and sometimes less complicated to keep track of.

In Table 7.1, you can see a typical task list using a spreadsheet to keep track of all the tasks. It's worth adding a new tab for each time you update the list so that you can refer back to tasks and see when they were first introduced and when they were completed in case of a future dispute. Each task has several pieces of information along with colour coding to identify if it is 'to do', 'in hand or ordered', or 'dependent' on another task that needs actioning as a priority. It's worth adding whether the task is critical (i.e. does another task depend on it). Technically, a task becomes critical when it goes onto the critical path. Think of the critical path as the shortest possible time that the project could take.

As a very simple example, imagine you are making pancakes. You are estimating that the whole task will take 20 minutes: 5 minutes to find the ingredients, 5 minutes to mix the ingredients and 10 minutes to cook the pancakes.

Each of those tasks is critical. If it takes longer to find the ingredients then the whole task will take more than 20 minutes. However, you could find that when it comes to cooking the pancakes you have to wash up the frying pan or you have run out of butter to cook with, then those unexpected tasks become critical and lengthen the critical path. If there's two of you, one of you may have to go and buy the butter while the other is preparing the batter. At that point, preparing the batter drops off the critical path and is replaced by buying the butter, which is the longer critical task.

For complex projects, this is really only trackable using software such as Microsoft Project.

Issue	Discussed (date)	Who	Comment / action	Critical	Deadline (date)	Notes
Fit boiler	1.05.22	Plumber	Waiting on roof penetration	Y	31.05.22	
Doors – missing hinges on 2 doors	15.04.22	Carpenter	Hinges on site	N	10.05.22	
Fit doors	14.6.22	Carpenter	Ordered	N	9.07.22	
Ironmongery	3.3.22	Carpenter	Order	N	10.04.22	Done
Light fitting for ground floor	15.3.22	Electrician	Long lead time, needs ordering	Y	1.04.22	Urgent

● to do ● done ● dependent ● waiting for delivery Highlight = priority

Table 7.1 A typical task list to keep track of what is required on site. Use colour coding to help understand whether a task is urgent, waiting for delivery, done, dependent on another task or outstanding.

You will have a task list that deals with delivery, but you may also want a tracker or task list that helps you to deal with all of the other tasks required of you as a developer, e.g. marketing, sales, planning, building regulations and legal documentation.

Ideally, you will generate a programme from your task lists, which will help you to keep on top of the required actions and should be reviewed daily or weekly, depending on the stage of the project. You need to keep your funders updated on a monthly or quarterly basis. On an annual basis, you will want to keep checks on all the various insurance that is needed both for yourself and the contractor and make sure they are all up to date.

In summary, you have a choice to make: you can run the project yourself, which has the advantage of being cheaper, giving you greater control and allowing you to learn as you go. However, if you make a fundamental mistake, it could end up costing more than you have saved. Moreover, it can absorb most of your time and so is only worth considering if you can commit the time to it. Alternatively, you can hire professionals to do it for you, which frees you up to do or start other projects but will take money away from the project's profitability.

CASE STUDY

PROJECT	Catching Sun House, London, UK
ARCHITECT DEVELOPER	Studioshaw
COMPLETION	2020

Mark Shaw established Studioshaw in 2016. Together with two architect friends, Greg Blee and Lee Halligan, they bought a plot at auction and built two houses, which they now live in. The site, in Walthamstow, east London, was a disused MOT garage surrounded on all sides by existing houses and gardens. Working to a tight budget, the architects managed the contract themselves. The build took just 11 months from start to finish.

The architects bought the site with planning for two houses but quickly realised they could increase the value. Shaw says, 'I didn't like the design and of course, being architects, we wanted to design something different.'[3]

They spent some time deciding on who was having which plot of land while also thinking about the designs of both houses. They agreed to split the demolition, clearance, foundations and the blockwork. Although the work was split into two packages, it still involved working out who was paying for what. Shaw says, 'There was a lot of doing spreadsheets late at night and actually, with hindsight, it maybe would have been worth having a QS just because it can easily get complicated. But there were no dramas.'

The initial plan was to clear the site, demolish the existing buildings, resolve the clay pipe sewers (which had to be removed), level it, clean the site and rebuild all the party walls. The contractor they hired for this impressed them so much with his precision that they gave him the blockwork package and began to think they could divide the work into packages using specialist contractors they had worked with in the past.

Although they hadn't planned to run the project without a main contractor, and it took 'time and energy' to work this way, it allowed them to go through each package with the subcontractor and go 'round and round on the details', until it was something they could afford.

Another advantage to this approach is that because they weren't having to issue all the information at the beginning of the project, they had a longer design time, which allowed them to refine and issue precise drawings for each package. But they were only able to work this way because they had used their own money to buy the land and then raised a self-build mortgage for the construction, which releases money in stages as the project progresses.

Figure 7.2 (above) Studioshaw, Catching Sun House, London. View of the main dining and living space. Materials are simple and exposed – concrete floors, blockwork walls and timber.

Figure 7.3 (below) Studioshaw, Catching Sun House, London. View of the living space from the adjacent main courtyard. A very high level of detailed design was done by the practice.

Figure 7.4 (above) Studioshaw, Catching Sun House, London. The windows of the west-facing living spaces by night.

Figure 7.5 (below) Studioshaw, Catching Sun House, London. View from the roof of the neighbouring house showing the building in its Victorian context. The west-facing facade catches the afternoon sunlight.

Figure 7.6 Studioshaw, Catching Sun House, London. The entrance to the house, viewed from the adjoining street.

Shaw explains, 'The downside of the packages approach is that you don't have anyone managing things on site. I was lucky with the builder that I used for most of the packages that he managed all of those. But when I brought in other subcontractors that were not under his jurisdiction, that's when the odd tension came out, because he knew he wasn't being paid an overhead kind of figure to manage that particular subcontractor.'

Shaw also used his experience of partnering contracts and giving the contractor the opportunity to properly look at the drawings before signing the contract so he could come back with comments and queries. He expands, 'They [the contractor] have to sign on the dotted line that they are 100% confident that they can do what's on these drawings for this price. And you say, "You're not allowed variations on this project." And every time they come back and they've added a bit more money on, so you say, "Are you 100% sure you can deliver this for this price?" And eventually they say, "Okay, let's do it."'

Shaw was determined not to go over his original budget of £400,000, so he built in a contingency to make sure each package cost less than the figure in the appraisal. He concludes, 'If I'm honest with myself, I spent a bit more on the house than I had in the development appraisal because of the things you forget about adding into appraisal like blinds and curtains and fitted furniture. There are lots of extra costs that creep in over time.'

Figure 7.7 Studioshaw, Catching Sun House, London. By removing the role of main contractor, the architect estimates he saved 20% on overheads and prelims and another 10% by controlling the tender process and 'value engineering' separate elements.

Figure 7.8 (above) Studioshaw, Catching Sun House, London. View of the kitchen and dining space.

Figure 7.9 (below) Studioshaw, Catching Sun House, London. Orange staircase leading to the first-floor office and living space. This space was carefully designed to give space for the MVHR system and air source heat pump.

CASE STUDY

PROJECT	Pop Brixton, London, UK
ARCHITECT DEVELOPER	Turner Works
COMPLETION	2015

Carl Turner is a London-based architect and founder of Turner Works. He built his own house, the award-winning Slip House, where he was living and running the studio from, but became frustrated that it had not led to bigger projects. As Turner says, 'I thought Slip House was going to open lots of doors, but I'd got on that hamster wheel of private residential work and I couldn't seem to get off.'[4]

Spotting that his local council was advertising for groups or organisations to come forward with ideas for 'meanwhile uses' for a piece of land in Brixton, he decided to pitch his idea for the site based around shipping containers, which he had built with before.

Turner was shortlisted and eventually selected. He says, 'I suppose for me it was a launchpad to really change the nature of the practice for the rest of my working life. I've described it as a kind of last chance saloon. I thought, if this doesn't work, I'll probably just go off and do the odd new-build house every two or three years and keep doing the kind of work I've been doing, so it was a game-changing opportunity.'

He had to sell Slip House because it was the only way to raise the capital and satisfy the council he had money in the bank. At that point, he took a lease from the council, with an initial deal for three years for the site. Turner explains, 'We had a really simple lease and then the heads of terms behind it were all of these kind of more detailed negotiations about all the good stuff that we would try and deliver on the site. So it was really a partnership with the council and we agreed on a 50% profit share. What this meant is that once all the costs were paid, we'd pay 50% of the profit to the council in lieu of rent. So it was quite a complex deal, quite innovative in terms of what the council did. I think Mary [Turner's partner] and I invested about £150,000 up front to start the work on site, which involved buying the first 30 or 40 shipping containers, because we wanted to build confidence and prove that it was going to start happening.'

Turner needed to find other investors who were interested in the project and met Reza Merchant, then CEO of The Collective. Merchant agreed initially to invest approximately £350,000 in the project in return for 50% of the shares. 'Initially I was the 100% owner of Pop Brixton, but as Reza invested more money he took more of the shareholding.'

Figure 7.10 Turner Works, Pop Brixton, London. The development is built from low-cost, low-energy shipping containers that have been tailored to bespoke specifications.

'What happened though was when the investors came in they immediately saw it as an opportunity to roll it out as a model. So the council then ran a competition for Peckham car park, which the team that delivered Pop Brixton pitched for and won.'

He set up a parent company to look after the different businesses but different priorities eventually got in the way and the investors bought him out. Turner doubled the money he had put in.

Although there were difficult times, Turner has no regrets. 'It's given us great experience and that kind of entrepreneurial spirit and an understanding of how these things work. At the moment I'm also operating another site called Coach Works in Ashford independently. We're not making a huge amount of money, but it's just demonstrating that these projects can work outside central London.'

Figure 7.11 Turner Works, Pop Brixton, London. The local council was trying to build confidence in Brixton so the architect felt it would be a good place to invest.

Figure 7.12 (above) Turner Works, Pop Brixton, London. The architect was attracted by the brief, which supported local talent as well as requiring him to have input into the development's ethos.

Figure 7.13 (below) Turner Works, Pop Brixton, London. The architect had to constantly review the budget during construction and come up with low-cost design solutions.

Figure 7.14 (above) Turner Works, Pop Brixton, London. Pop Brixton has transformed a derelict space into a hive of activity bringing much-needed affordable work and leisure spaces to the area.

Figure 7.15 (below) Turner Works, Pop Brixton, London. Pop Brixton under construction. The architect had experience working with shipping containers and as a contractor on other projects.

CHAPTER 8
MARKETING AND SALES

In our penultimate chapter we look at how you market and sell what you've just spent years buying, designing, financing and building. Many developers take the 'if you build it, they will come' attitude, which is fine if you are happy to sell at the same price as everything else on the market. However, if you have spent more money on better design or quality, or if you have made the building more sustainable and environmentally friendly, you will want – and maybe need – a premium. That's where marketing and sales comes in.

Out of all the steps you must take on your development journey, marketing is probably the least understood. Put simply: architects have never really understood the value of marketing and many practices continue to view marketing activity as an expensive and unnecessary appendage.

Although Maria Sjölander and Marco da Cruz (see chapter 4) have never had to work hard to find buyers – such is the demand for their developments – they have now reached a point where they see the need for marketing support. 'We're learning that as you go on, you have to get the message out and you have to identify yourself and your difference very articulately. We're starting to enter that world of competing with developers who are getting more savvy about markets as well,' says da Cruz.[1]

You have a couple of choices when it comes to marketing and selling – you can choose to do some or all of it yourself, or you can outsource both activities. In the first section of this chapter we will look at what you need to consider when you are outsourcing this activity and in the second section we will give you the things you need to think about when you are doing it yourself.

OUTSOURCING MARKETING AND SALES

When you are paying someone else to do this work, the critical thing is to find someone who shares your design values and understands your vision.

For a small development (say fewer than five homes) you don't need to overthink this and you can probably wait until the end of the development, take some good photos, dress one of the flats and find a good agent to sell them.

If you are doing a larger development, you should consider off-plan sales and bringing a specialist marketing and sales consultant on board.

Before starting the sales process you should ideally have all your legal documents in order. If you're building flats, you will need to consider things like whether you will be selling leasehold or share of freehold. Until recently, developers have sold their homes as leasehold and then sold on the freehold as a way to make an extra few thousand pounds on each development. We would encourage you to avoid creating leaseholds as buyers are generally avoiding them and legislation is changing to give leaseholders more power. If you're building houses, you may also have to set up a management company and decide what that manages.

HOW TO CHOOSE AN AGENT

You now have a variety of options as to how you sell your property. Do you work with a high-street agent, an online agent, a niche agent, or do you do it yourself?

Like everything, there are pros and cons to each. The key is to pick the route that is most closely aligned to your market. Don't pick a local agent if you are selling something design-led and at a premium. If they don't understand the product then neither will your prospective customers. Instead, it would be better to find an agent who is more used to selling higher-end homes. Ask for references and look at other properties that they have sold recently. If they provide you with properties that are not comparable to yours from a design perspective, look elsewhere.

There are a growing number of agents who focus on selling design-led homes, the most famous and biggest of which is London-based The Modern House.[2] However they are selective in the areas that they operate and don't do off-plan sales so are best used if you are doing smaller developments. If you can't find a suitably design-minded agent to help you, you may have to approach a national agent or consider doing some of the agency work yourself.

Donald Matheson, who sold two flats as part of his development in Forest Gate (see chapter 5), says that while he did use a local agent, they were only ever offering the properties to people looking in that area while 'the thing about The Modern House is that somebody might see the flats and be interested but it had never occurred to them to move to the area. What they wanted was to live in a particular type of space ... something a little bit different.'[3]

Sometimes, you may have to sell with the same agent you bought the land from. You may end up finding this rather unsatisfactory if you are trying to sell something different and so, if you do sign up to that agreement at the beginning of a project, make sure you are allowed to bring on a second agent of your choice either immediately or after an initial 'lock-in' exclusivity period.

You should also be aware of the agency problem. This is where an agent's interests and your interests are not aligned. On first appearances you would have thought that you and your agent want the same thing – to sell the property for the highest price – wrong! You want to sell the property for the highest price, but the agent just wants to sell the property for whatever price they can in the shortest time possible.

Imagine that you are selling a £1,000,000 house. The agent has offered to sell it for you for 2%, which means their fee is £20,000. Now imagine that it doesn't sell quickly. Two months later the agent will be emailing you to tell you that it's priced too high and you should put the price down to £900,000. Even though the agent is on a commission, you are not aligned. You have just wiped £100,000 from your revenue (£1,000,000 - £900,000), which directly reduces your profitability of the project. In the meantime, the agent's commission has reduced from 2% of £1,000,000 (£20,000) to 2% of £900,000 (£18,000), and they have only lost a mere £2,000.

Be aware that certain agents use this problem to their advantage and value properties much higher than they are worth to gain the instruction. Once the instruction is gained, you are locked in and the agent has control of the situation for three months. The more properties an agent has on their books, the more control they have of the market and the more likely they are to make a sale – also known as the networking effect. That's good for them but not necessarily good for you.

To mitigate this, try to make the agent's contract as short as possible so that if they are unsuccessful you can approach other agents. You can also create incentives for them selling at a higher price. For example, you can try to negotiate a 1.5% sales fee if they sell for £900,000 and 2.5% if they sell for £1,000,000. You can never completely avoid the agency problem but at least you are now aware of it.

DOING MARKETING AND SALES IN-HOUSE

Doing the marketing and sales yourself is less scary than you think and very achievable for architect developers. You will probably have the skill set and the software to create better marketing collateral than an agent could produce. You will also know your homes inside-out and be more knowledgeable than an agent when conducting viewings.

However, doing it yourself requires an understanding of how marketing and sales actually work and the rest of the chapter is an overview.

THE SPANCO MODEL

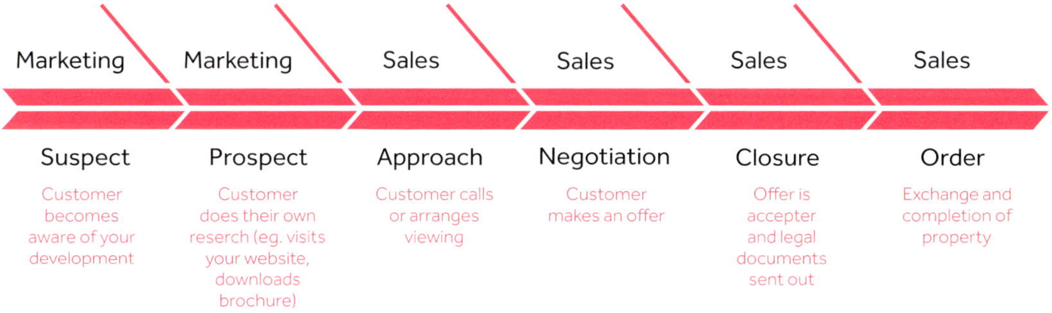

Figure 8.1 The SPANCO Model – every purchase will move along this funnel even if they go through some stages quickly.

There are many theoretical models of marketing and selling, but they all work on the same principle. Customers start at the large end of a 'funnel' and work their way down until they get to the small end, when they make the purchase. The reason we use the funnel analogy is that it narrows from top to bottom which mirrors the way potential customers drop out at every stage of the sales process and the actual number of buyers is a small percentage of the interested potential customers at the top of the funnel.[4]

There are always huge numbers of people looking for new homes, but more than 99.9% of them will not buy your homes because of any number of factors including location, budget or just not liking what you've built.

Marketing deals with the first two stages in the SPANCO model, which is making potential customers aware of your homes and encouraging them to make an enquiry. Sales deals with the latter four stages, until the offer is made and paid for.

Our top tip is to keep track of your customers, either using an Excel spreadsheet or one of many free customer relation management (CRM) tools while making sure you follow General Data Protection Regulations. You will need to follow up with customers throughout their journey and encourage them to take the next step in the funnel. Also, make sure that every email or touch point ends with a 'call to action' so that your potential customers know what to do next.

Suspect

The first stage is when a potential customer is looking for a property and becomes aware of your homes. Some 90% of the time, customers will find you through one of the property portals, so if you are doing this yourself, you will either need to sign up to a 'developer package', which will allow you to use your branding (but is expensive), or find an online agent who lists your property for you for a smaller fee.

Prospect

This is the second stage of SPANCO. You should expect to convert approximately one person in every 100 into an enquiry. To increase your conversion rate on the portals make sure you create a fantastic listing. You will need great photos, understandable plans and easy-to-understand content.

It's not just the portals: all of your channels, including your website and your social media presence, are ways to generate enquiries so make sure you make good use of them.

Approach

Treat every enquiry with kid gloves and respond quickly and professionally. You should be aiming to get about one viewing or meeting (if you're selling off-plan) from every five enquiries.

When you get the viewing or meeting this is when sales kicks in. Don't think of sales as a dirty activity, it doesn't need to be. Be authentic, professional and treat your potential customer how you would want to be treated. Have open and honest conversations about why your properties would work for your customer. Always think about it from their perspective and don't be afraid to say that you don't think it would be for them if you don't. Your customers will respect you more if you're honest. It's worth having a pre-viewing conversation to establish budgets and needs of your potential customer so that you don't waste your time (or theirs).

You've lived and breathed the designs for months if not years at this stage, so on the viewing point out the details you're proud of and why you designed it the way you did and focus on the benefits to the customer. If they ask you a question you don't know the answer to, don't fob them off or lie, be honest and say you don't know but you'll let them know and then make sure you get back to them.

Negotiation

You should be aiming to get one offer from every five to 10 viewings. It's now down to your negotiation skills (more later) whether you accept the first offer or get them to improve it. If you have had several offers, be clear about the process. Sealed bids are a common way to make it fair for everyone.

Closure

If you do get an offer you may need to speak to your bank before you accept it. Note that about 50% of offers fall through so you may want your customer to pay a reservation fee to disincentivise them from pulling out. If you do want to do this, make sure that the fee is paid directly from their solicitor to yours so that you don't have to deal with anti-money-laundering regulations.

If you are selling newly built homes you will now have to provide a ream of information about the development including building regulation approval, plans and planning approval to various parties including mortgage valuers and lawyers. It's wise to have all this information easily to hand as it will be requested frequently.

Order

In this context, 'Order' means that you have exchanged contracts. Unfortunately, you probably won't see any of that money until you've sold all but the last one or two homes in your development, as the first sales go directly to pay back the bank for their loan.

WHAT COLLATERAL DO YOU NEED AND WHO WILL DO IT?

Depending on the size of your development, you will need some or all of the following:

- **Website** – if your website has decent traffic and you are using Google Analytics or other third-party tools, it makes sense to add your development rather than go to the expense of a stand-alone website. If you do need a stand-alone website, use one of the free design and web hosting tools to create something inexpensive.
- **Brochure** – hard-copy brochures are lovely, but expensive and not necessary for smaller developments. Instead, you may want to think about an e-brochure, which takes time to design but can really help with converting leads to enquiries (suspects to prospects).
- **Computer-generated images (CGIs)** – if you are doing off-plan sales CGIs are now essential. One tip is that virtual staging is much cheaper than CGIs if you have photographs.
- **Plans and specification** – you will also need to tell your customers what they are buying so they can make an informed choice. 2D plans can still be hard for customers to read so you may want to invest in 3D plans.
- **Virtual tours** – while the building is being constructed you cannot give someone an actual tour, but the technology for CGI virtual tours is becoming better and helps customers understand what they are buying.
- **Miscellaneous** – there is a host of other marketing collateral that you could commission – from 3D-printed models, to tote bags and keyrings. You will have to consider your audience and work out what it is they would value and how they want to remember or understand the development and your company.

Many architectural software packages now have the ability to do a lot of the CGI and virtual tours and you may be used to putting planning documents together. If you have the skill set and capacity, it's well worth you considering doing some or all of the marketing collateral.

Top tip: benefits vs features

Always communicate the 'benefits' to your customer, not your home's 'features' – i.e. don't tell them how your home is highly insulated (feature), tell them that it will reduce their heating bills (benefit).

The more you understand your customer, the more you can talk their language in all your marketing collateral and content and explain the benefits that will make your homes stand out.

WHAT CHANNELS SHOULD YOU USE TO GET ENQUIRIES?

Apart from the portals, there are a few other places where people can find you:

- **Hoarding for people walking by** – many people stay local when they move house so don't underestimate the power of a good hoarding.
- **Local leafleting in shops** – leafleting is often more effective in smaller communities.
- **Social media** – social media marketing is a book in itself but the key here is consistency. Pick your platform of choice and make sure you stick with it throughout the development. Don't do a flurry of posts and then nothing. Building a following takes time and regular posting, and there are no shortcuts.
- **Press** – press gives you credibility and reach. You may have contacts to help you, otherwise seek out a PR who will have the contacts to get you noticed.
- **Newsletters/website/search engine optimization (SEO)** – newsletters are an excellent way of building buzz and excitement and a great way to keep communication during the journey. SEO creates new leads but requires investment of time to create good content.
- **Local sponsorship** – if you are targeting local families, sponsor a raffle competition at the local school for example.
- **Advertising** – a simple but expensive way to get your message out there and make people aware of your homes. As this is expensive it only really makes sense for larger developments.

Unfortunately, all of these approaches can cost money and take time and you don't know which one will yield success. As the great marketeer John Wanamaker said, 'Half of the money I spend on marketing is wasted. The trouble is, I don't know which half.'

HOW MUCH ARE THE HOMES?

Of course, you can always invite agents to give you a free valuation on your homes. However, these days, you can also do your own research on the property portals. You will need to think about the pricing carefully. Too high and buyers will be priced out, too low and you will be leaving money on the table.

Buyers generally look in budget brackets, as that is how the portals list properties, so try to price so that you are in two brackets. For example, price your home at £650,000, which would appear in searches for both £600,000–£650,000 and £650,000–£700,000.

WHAT SHOULD THE HOMES LOOK LIKE?

When you first found the site, you will have looked at the area. Now you are designing the homes, or deciding on the fit-out, you need to understand the customer. Your goal is to build up a detailed picture of who your customer is likely to be – this is known in marketing speak as the 'avatar'. The more detailed the picture, the easier it will be both to design the home and market it. You should have two to three avatars for every development. You need to really understand who lives or aspires to live in the area. Some things to consider are:

- Will your buyers be a large family, an aspiring family or downsizing?
- What is the typical housing stock – is it large or small housing, flats or maisonettes, new-build or post-war estates?
- What age will they be?
- What are the local facilities and local schools – are there obvious signs of downsizers in the area or is the school run very busy?
- Are your buyers design-orientated?
- What is the style of local shops and cafes; they are generally a good indicator of what their clientele wants. Are they 'greasy spoons' or upmarket coffee bars? Are the shops independent or discount supermarkets?
- Will your buyers be working from home?
- How busy is the commute at the local transport hub? Are the local cafes full of people on their laptops?
- Will your buyers want large entertainment spaces? Families tend to like to dine-in, but young professionals may prefer to eat out.
- Do your buyers care about sustainability?
- Is there any evidence from the shops and restaurants of an interest in sustainable living? Are there lots of bike shops around?

Don't be afraid of chatting to cafe owners and local shop owners, asking them about their customers. This is what Sophie Goldhill did when working out what kind of rents local businesses would be prepared to pay (see chapter 1).[5] The more information you can gather, the more likely you are to build something that really solves your target market's problems and will then sell for a premium.

WHEN DO YOU START MARKETING AND SELLING?

You have a choice to sell off-plan, wait until your development is built or do a hybrid. If you are selling more than three or four homes, selling some off-plan is a sensible approach to reducing your exposure at the end of the development. Some banks may even require it.

Do not underestimate how long it takes to sell a home once it's finished; if you can sell some, or all, of your development by the time you have finished building, your cash flow and bank will thank you for it. The advantage of off-plan sales is that within 10 days of practical completion (PC) of your development, you will have that money in the bank, or, more likely, you will have repaid your funder. At the end of the project, as you will have drawn down all your funds, your interest costs will be running at eye-watering rates, typically thousands of pounds every week which will be eating into your profit.[6]

You can start your marketing and making people aware of your homes as soon as you have secured planning permission and have a contractor in place. Register interest and keep in touch with your potential customers with newsletters, video diaries and social media posts.

However, it's best to wait until about six months before completion before you officially launch the sales. If you launch too early customers can get excited and then frustrated if you get delayed and mortgage offers only tend to stay open for three to six months. Make sure you have your legal documents in place before you launch.

OFF-PLAN SELLING

On the whole, people are naturally fearful of change or things they don't know. They trust what they see with their own eyes and/or what they hear from trusted friends or colleagues. This means that if you are trying to sell your homes before they are built (which is good for your cash flow), your job will be extra hard; you have to build up trust with your potential customers and deliver on your promises. If you are reading this book, you are unlikely to be running a branded house builder, so you will need to think about how to build up trust in other ways. For example, if you are an established practice who have decided to set up a development arm, you already have an existing client base and you should let them know that you are now doing your own developments as they or their friends may be your future purchasers.

HOW TO NEGOTIATE

Part of selling is knowing how to negotiate. There are many books on this subject, so if you are going to be doing your own negotiation you may wish to read up, but in the meantime, here are a few pointers.[7]

BATNA and ZOPA

These are two terms that every negotiator should know about. ZOPA is the 'Zone of Potential Agreement'. This means that if you are willing to sell your house for £950,000 at the very minimum, and the buyer is willing to pay up to £975,000 at the very most, your ZOPA is £975,000 minus £950,000 = £25,000.

However, if you aren't prepared to sell for less than £1,000,000 then there is no ZOPA. Unfortunately, there is no easy way to find out your buyer's absolute maximum, which is where negotiation comes in and where you have to be a detective to gather as much information as possible.

BATNA stands for 'Best Alternative to a Negotiated Agreement', which in essence means what other options do you and your buyer have. If your buyer has to be in a certain catchment area for their children and your house is the only one available in that area, then their BATNA is very weak. If they don't buy your house they'd have to rent, or change their plans for their children, or wait and hope for the best.

On the other hand, if your development is a two-bed flat in a market full of other two-bed flats, then your buyer's BATNA is very strong.

The same is true for you as a seller. If this buyer walks away, do you have lots of other offers or potential purchasers? Or have you had only one enquiry in the last month?

These are all closely guarded pieces of information and so, the more you can find out about your buyer, the better position you will be in as a negotiator.

In summary, marketing and sales are something that you should be aware of from the beginning and you should have a strategy for how you want to deal with them. If you get it wrong, all that hard work can be undone and you can lose valuable profitability and credibility with your backers. Get it right and you will be set for the next project.

CASE STUDY

PROJECT	RAW Rosendal, Uppsala, Sweden
ARCHITECT DEVELOPER	RAW Property
COMPLETION	2022

Oliver Thornton moved to Sweden in 2007. In 2012 he set up a practice with architect Johan Berg and together they developed their own concept of contemporary shell homes. To realise their ambition, they founded RAW Property, which subsequently entered into a joint venture with a well-known Swedish housebuilder. After completing and selling its first scheme in Uppsala in 2022, RAW is now building in three cities across Sweden, including Stockholm.

In Sweden, a lot of land is controlled by local councils, who block buy big sites and put in all the infrastructure and do the development, explains Thornton. But this does not make it any easier for a small developer. Although around half of this housing land is sold by councils, the competition for sites is intense. 'Lots of people want to do it and the main barrier to entry is money' he adds.[8]

Thornton's pitch was to say, 'Look, you're building all this housing, which is great, but most of it is pretty much the same stuff – it's a little bit more luxurious or a little bit simpler – but we have a product that is completely different. It attracts a different kind of buyer. And we have lots of socially sustainable ideas behind building these shell homes.'

Once the two architects had been offered a site by the council in Uppsala, they founded the company. They had a land option for two years to buy the land but at that point they didn't have funding for the whole project.

Confident they would be able to raise the finance, they began to design the scheme. They also began to market the apartments as a proof of concept at the same time as making sure that the project satisfied the local planners.

Thornton explains, 'It was slow at the start because we were in a difficult market. In 2017/2018 there was a dip in Sweden and we came in at the end of that, but one good thing was we didn't have much competition. There were not many other people building in that city at the time, but it was difficult. We worked on the sales for the rest of that year.'

They had a local estate agent but produced all of the sales material themselves driving up to Uppsala every Monday evening for open evenings at the estate agent where they met potential clients. They were also advertising on social media and the Swedish equivalent of Rightmove, called Hemnet.

Figure 8.2 Johan Berg Arkitekter, RAW Rosendal, Uppsala. The project is the architect developer's first and is based on the concept of 'raw' flexible space. It comprises 50 apartments and three commercial units.

Figure 8.3 (above) Johan Berg Arkitekter, RAW Rosendal, Uppsala. The largest apartment offers the possibility of inserting a second floor. Most buyers have chosen to preserve a section of the double-height space.

Figure 8.4 (below) Johan Berg Arkitekter, RAW Rosendal, Uppsala. Window sizes are calculated to allow for a flexible layout. All homes are delivered with a complete bathroom and a simple kitchen.

By the end of 2019 they had sold a few apartments. They had also signed a land option for a second project as well as a site in Stockholm. Suddenly, it went from one little project to potentially three projects.

Thornton says, 'We were battling to get through one project so doing three was impossible. At that point we had to decide if we wanted to just say no to the other two and keep going on the first project or push on forwards and try to expand. And we decided to do the latter, so we found a partner, who is a well-established Stockholm and Uppsala housebuilder, and a listed company who've been building housing since the 1980s.'

The housebuilder ended up taking the controlling share of the company, buying 51% of RAW and, in doing so, transforming their financing situation. Thornton moved to become CEO of RAW within the new ownership structure, while his former partner, Berg, stayed at the practice and was the architect for the first development in Uppsala.

Thornton reflects, 'I'm not someone who went to architecture school because I had a calling in life that I am an architect. I did it because I think it's really interesting. And I loved it and I was passionate about my job at the time and I was running an architectural practice in Sweden. But now I'm doing this, and this is exciting, and I'm learning new things.'

Figure 8.5 Johan Berg Arkitekter, RAW Rosendal, Uppsala. A primary steel beam system allows for the installation of a second floor in all loft apartments.

Figure 8.6 Johan Berg Arkitekter, RAW Rosendal, Uppsala. Nearly all owners have chosen to preserve some untreated concrete in their homes.

CASE STUDY

PROJECT	495 West Street, New York, USA
ARCHITECT DEVELOPER	Tamarkin Co.
COMPLETION	1999

Cary Tamarkin has designed and developed almost a dozen properties in Manhattan. He is generally credited with bringing raw space back into vogue after it had fallen out of favour a decade or so earlier. His first project was 140 Perry Street, a 1920s warehouse building in Greenwich Village, which he bought in 1995.

Now retired and living in Shelter Island New York his advice to architects starting their property journey is to find a niche as he did: spotting the potential of Manhattan's dormant factories and warehouses at a time when the city was becoming safer and cleaner and families and others were seeking large amounts of space.

Tamarkin explains, 'I was 35 years old working until two in the morning every day. I loved it, but I needed to ask my girlfriend to marry me and I wanted to have some kids. I wanted to have a nice life, so I threw everything in the air. I said to myself, "If I was not going to be an architect, what do I think I could be good at and make some money?" I just took it all away, which is a great thing to do a couple of times in your lifetime.'[9]

In 1991 at the end of a long recession, Tamarkin walked around his home neighbourhood of Tribeca and West Village for about six months, looking at buildings and for an opportunity. Developers were struggling so he decided to try to meet with any of them that would see him.

Tamarkin found a building at 140 Perry Street – the same street where he lived – which he describes as an old concrete warehouse with 16ft-high ceilings, striking beams and 'great bones for development'. But the area was down at heel. 'It was kind of scary to even walk there at night. I made a list of about 100 people that I thought I could raise money from and I got to the fourth person on the list, who is a good friend of mine, and I took him out to dinner. He had just been made the head of real estate of Oaktree Capital Management, which is a multi-billion-dollar fund. I said I needed US$4,000,000, which seemed like a ton of money, and he said, "Forget about your father, your stepfather. Forget about the banks. We're putting in US$4,000,000 and you're going to pass a 35% rate of return and if there's anything left after that, we'll split it." So I did this project, worked like crazy, it was really nuts. Anyway, everything sold in two seconds. There was US$2,000,000 extra and I made a million bucks. I had never thought of US$1,000,000. I had never seen US$1,000,000 so things were off to a good start.'

With his first development under his belt, Tamarkin continued working with the same investor, specialising in old warehouses delivered as raw space apartments or 'condos'.

He explains, 'The next three or four buildings I did were all delivered as raw space and that turned out to be a good idea because I figured that while there were fewer people that wanted that, those people that did want it had fewer places to find it. And that was kind of an idea through my whole career as a developer.'

He went on to act as both developer and architect for a string of other high-profile projects including 495 West Street, a new-build project, again with open raw-space interiors and panoramic views of the Hudson River.

Tamarkin concludes, 'I wouldn't do a project unless it had a chance of being a beautiful building. And I wouldn't do a project unless it had a chance of making a lot of money. So that was a constant battle. I definitely could have made more money if I chose to do things as cheaply as possible, but I wouldn't do that. I didn't want to do that. I genuinely care about the city and I care about the buildings that I leave the city, and that's just the way it is.'

Figure 8.7 CT Architect, 495 West Street, New York. The architect describes his development on the Hudson River as his favourite building. The 11-storey new-build consists of nine apartments, two of them duplex penthouses.

Figure 8.8 CT Architect, 495 West Street, New York. After a series of successful conversions, the architect embarked on his first new-build while staying true to New York's warehouse aesthetic.

Figure 8.9 CT Architect, 495 West Street, New York. Large industrial steel grid windows face west, providing Hudson River views.

CHAPTER 9
STARTING THE JOURNEY

Over the course of this book we have emphasised the risk that development poses every step of the way, but also the satisfaction that comes from making your own projects and being your own boss.

All the architects we've interviewed have found a path through the jungle and have come out the other side. Either they've returned to architecture full-time or have reshaped their practice so they can look for new opportunities.

This suggests that development is not just something architects can do successfully, but a pursuit they can also enjoy. More important is the financial reward and the satisfaction of knowing you are creating a product people are prepared to pay for.

The case studies in the book might encourage you to take the plunge. Equally, you may have reached this chapter and thought 'this is not for me'. But if your takeaway is a greater understanding of your clients' pain points then that is no bad thing. The architect/client relationship is often fraught because the architect does not understand the complexity of the developer's role; we hope that this book has made that role a bit clearer.

If you still harbour ambitions to be an architect developer, our advice is action rather than waiting for the stars to align, because in property development they never will.

So, the big question is when to start on this journey, because as any successful entrepreneur will tell you, ideas are nothing if they remain ideas.

Some would-be architect developers will tell you that they are waiting for the perfect site to fall into their lap, but it rarely does. Others spend years looking for an investor willing to back them while worrying about the state of the economy. Nearly everyone scours the internet for advice. There is nothing wrong with this but if you are serious about becoming an architect developer, you will need to get your hands dirty.

That's not to say you shouldn't do your research first. But remember that no time is ever perfect, and the property industry likes nothing better than making predictions about the next crash and what might, or might not, happen in the future. As Cary Tamarkin put it, 'If you're smart enough, you can do the analysis and figure out where the economy is headed, but it's always a guess.'[1] And it can be lonely. There's no professional body for developers ready to give you support and no matter how good your idea, no one can build a new business by themselves. You need to find people to share your vision, complement your skills and help keep things in perspective.

So, this chapter is about some practical steps to help you get started, because once you're on your way, you will find that development has its own rhythm, much of which will be familiar, except now you are the one in charge and holding the reins.

STEP 1: LEARN

The first step is to carry on learning. If you've read this book and come this far, then you already know more than many others. Have a look at property courses either online or in person and start networking. Join property networking events in your area and build your network of agents and finance brokers, but don't stop there. Speak to other property professionals as you never know where the conversation will lead. In this industry, you have to kiss a lot of frogs.

STEP 2: FIND LAND

Over the past few years it has become easier to find and research land opportunities online. Online property portals, auction websites and Government open data all mean that you can find and learn everything about a site relatively quickly – from ownership and planning history to historic sales values and future local plans – when it used to take weeks, even months, to gather all this information in person.

You can either collate various sources yourself or there are subscription services that mean you can access them all in one place. Although various attempts have been made to produce a comprehensive register of public land that can be accessed easily and for free they are almost always out of date and inaccurate. Local authorities do not have the time or resources to identify sites and they are not incentivised to do so because small developments bring few advantages in terms of affordable housing or amenities.

STEP 3: FIND MONEY

Financial technology or 'fintech', as it is better known, can also help if you are looking for funding. There is a plethora of new firms who have made it easier than ever to raise money. They are either brokers or crowdfunding platforms so try to develop a relationship with the ones you feel are a cultural fit.

Your biggest challenge will be to convince lenders that you are a worthy borrower. You don't have a track record (yet) so your first project will be the most difficult to get started. Don't forget that while it's hard to get the first project off the ground, every architect developer before you has managed to do it, and with persistence you will too. Find the opportunity, work the network and you'll find the money you need.

For example, one property may have a very high pound per square foot price because it has amazing views. New builds also normally have an approximate 10% premium over second-hand homes. Another may be cheap because it's in particularly bad condition, or there's an issue around the length of the lease, or it cannot be mortgaged for example. So just make sure you pick good comparable properties to give you an accurate sense of what you think you can sell your flats or units for. It's also generally the case that as a property's size increases, the pounds per square foot rate reduces and as a property becomes smaller, the pounds per square foot goes up. So, it's worth making sure you are comparing like with like or you may end up with a wildly inaccurate estimated GDV.

Table A1.01 shows an example of how to calculate your comparable values. It is worth having a link to the listing and the name of the agent. The average will help you to understand the typical stock in the area. This may give you an indication of what you should be building – you could consider building more of the same or build something that is not as easily available.

Comparable name	Date found	Type	Price	Ft^2	Price per ft^2	Beds	Status	Agent	Notes	Link
15 Anywhere Street	XXX[2]	House	850,000	1,500	567	4	Sold	XXX	Victorian terrace – needs modernising	XXX
52 Another Place	XXX	House	750,000	1,300	577	3	Unsold	XXX	Victorian terrace – recently refurbished	XXX
32 Random Mews	XXX	House	800,000	1,400	571	4	Sold	XXX	Victorian terrace – nice garden	XXX
Average			**800,000**	**1,400**	**572**	**3.7**				

Table A1.1 Calculation of £ per ft^2 for the area

SCHEDULE OF AREAS

Once you have a clear idea about how much the average pound per square foot is for the area, you should list in a sales tab the number of units and the saleable square footage of each, which gives you your total net square foot or net saleable area (NSA).

As well as NSA, you need to work out the square footage of the common parts – the lobby, bin stores and all those areas that people need but won't pay for, which together add to the Gross Internal Area (GIA).

Table A1.02 shows a schedule of areas. We use the price per square foot calculated from the comparable properties tab and apply it to each of our proposed units. In this example, we are building three houses. As they back onto the rail track, we are discounting them a little from a typical new-build premium. This is just a starting point; you will finesse these sales values over time with an agent or by keeping close watch on the market. As we are selling houses, the GIA and the NSA are the same. This would not be the case for flats as GIA includes common parts.

Unit	Beds	GIA sqm²	GIA sqft²	NET sqm² (NSA)	NET sqft² (NSA)	Price psf²	Sales
House 1	5.00	144	1,553	144	1,553	575	893,116
House 2	4.00	120	1,287	120	1,287	580	746,677
House 3	3.00	97	1,041	97	1,041	590	614,118
Total		**361**	**3,881**	**360.60**	**3,881**		**2,253,912**

Table A1.2 Calculation of GDV

Now we have estimated the GDV, we can start filling out the appraisal.

Please note that the appraisal is based on a mix of formulas and inputs. The numbers that you need to change are the inputs which are highlighted in yellow.

PURCHASE PRICE

Purchase		% purchase	Cost (£)
Purchase price			600,000
Stamp duty[3]	Commercial rate	3.3%	19,500
Legal fees – purchase			2,500
Other purchase costs			1,000
Seller's legal fees			0
Acquisition fee		2%	12,000
Total purchase price			**635,000**

Please use one of the many free Stamp Duty calculators you can find online.

Table A1.3 Typical purchase price costs

At this stage, we still don't know what the purchase price should be, so you can either use the guide price from the agent, make a guess, or take a rough 30% of the GDV as a starting point. This is often used as a rough rule of thumb for land that needs planning permission; it may be as high as 45–50% if it is land with planning permission. Refurbishment buildings are also going to be higher as a % of GDV.

The first question is whether this is a commercial or residential purchase because this affects the amount of stamp duty. If you are buying land (even if it's for a residential development), it's generally considered commercial land and you pay commercial rates for stamp duty. If you are unsure, you'll need to speak to your lawyer or a stamp duty specialist. You can find plenty of stamp duty calculators online. One way to minimise your stamp duty is if the land sits in a company (a Special Purpose Vehicle – SPV). If so, you can buy the 'company', which at time of writing attracts only 0.5% stamp duty rather than 4–5% for the asset. However, it does have downsides as you have to undertake more legal due diligence to make sure that the company has not been doing anything you will then be held liable for. If in doubt, seek advice from your lawyer and accountant.

If you have sourced your land through a land finder you will generally have to pay 2% of the land price as a finder's fee.

PLANNING COSTS

Table A1.04 shows typical costs to get to planning permission. Since it is your development, you can do away with both architectural and development management fees. This brings your costs down and allows you to bid more for the project. However, if you are working on a larger development with investors, you may wish to charge them for both your development management role and your architectural role.

The list below is a fairly comprehensive list of potential costs that a Local Authority may ask for but these will change all the time and other surveys may be required in your area. You can sometimes find out a list of what is required by either talking to the Local Authority, going on their website, or getting some clarity via the pre-application process.

It is well worth spending more money on higher quality information pre-planning if you can afford to. Your appraisal should include expenses you may incur to inform the design and costs pre-planning. For example, the input of an engineer or quantity surveyor may help you to decide what structure you wish to go for and what windows you wish to specify, which may impact on the planning of the interior and the exterior and the viability of the project. The more you spend upfront, the quicker you can get on site and get building. The downside is that if you don't get planning permission, that money will be wasted.

Planning costs	% construction	Cost (£)
Architectural fee	0.0%	0
Development management fee	0.0%	0
Fire consultant		1,000
Pre-construction CDM fee		500
Pre-planning QS work		500
Pre-planning engineers work		500
Air quality assessment		-
Arboricultural		1,000
Archeology		500
Land contamination (desk)		500
Noise and vibration		1,000
Planning consultant		2,500
Community engagement		-
Planning pre-app		1,500
Planning Submission	500 (per unit)	1,500
Rights to light		-
Sustainability report		-
Topographical survey		500
Miscellaneous		2,500
Total planning costs		**14,000**

Table A1.4 Typical planning costs you should consider or allow for

PRE-TENDER COSTS

Pre-tender costs	Cost (£)
Soil investigation	5,000
Contamination investigation	inc
Pre-Contract Service Agreement QS work (PCSA)	-
Pre-tender planning work	1,500
Pre-tender engineer's work	1,500
Archaeological investigation	-
Ecology	0
Drainage survey	1,000
Total pre-tender costs	**9,000**

Table A1.5 Typical costs you will pay before going to tender

Pre-tender costs are costs that will help you get a better and more reliable fixed price when you go to tender. For example, if you don't have a full soil analysis, including whether there is any contamination, your contractor won't be able to properly price up your foundations or the cost of earth excavation. The cost of removing contaminated soil is five to 10 times more expensive than uncontaminated soil.

POST-PLANNING COSTS

Fees after planning	% construction	Cost psm^2	Cost (£)
Architect	0.0%		-
Engineer	1.0%		8,016
QS & contract admin	1.0%		8,016
M&E	1.0%		8,016
Development management	0.0%		-
Sustainability			-
Building control fees			2,500
Building warranty	0.5% (of sales)		11,270
Construction CDM			1,000
Section 106			5,000

Fees after planning	% construction	Cost psm^2	Cost (£)
Community Infrastructure Levy (CIL)		50	37,275
Mayor Community Infrastructure Levy CIL		35	26,093
Affordable offset/viability			-
Legal fees/other costs for S.106			5,000
Acoustics			2,500
Scaffold license			10,000
Party walls			5,000
Network Rail/TFL license			20,000
Landscape architect			1,500
Insurance			2,000
Surveys			5,000
Total fees after planning			**158,184**

CIL costs are complicated and need to be looked at on a case-by-case basis. They are driven by the amount of new net area you are building and where it is being built.

Table A1.6 Post-planning fees and costs

CONSTRUCTION COSTS

	% construction	Cost per m^2	Cost (£)
Construction costs		2,000	721,200
Demolition & landscaping			7,500
Abnormals			-
Contingencies	10%		72,870
Total construction costs		**2,223**	**801,570**

Table A1.7 Construction costs

Since you won't have a huge amount of detail, your analysis of construction costs will probably be on a rate per square foot or per square metre of your GIA.

It's worth adding in any abnormal factors that may make your scheme more expensive. This may include site location (next to infrastructure, difficult access, far from services, sloping site) or structure (difficult ground conditions, complicated engineering) or design (high performance windows).

At this stage a healthy 10% contingency is a must. This can be reduced as you go through the project and the risk diminishes.

Table A1.08 shows some of the other costs you may encounter during the construction phase.

A scaffold licence is required when you do not have the right to put scaffolding on somebody else's land. If you are building in a city this is very common. However, you do have the right to put scaffolding on your neighbour's land when you're building right up to the boundary. Bear this in mind when you are designing the building as a scaffold licence can cost tens of thousands and take many months to organise and agree.

In cities, you may not need a scaffold licence but you will almost certainly need a party wall award. The good news is that there is an established process under the Party Wall Act. The bad news is that it can be expensive. It takes a lot of time and effort and you have to pay not only for your costs, but also for the costs of your neighbour. If you're dealing with any statutory body it will charge you for a top flight party wall surveyor firm and may also charge you for a 'checking engineer' to check your engineer's calculations. Party walls can get complicated when people fail to reply or when there is a block of flats next door, as you have to serve notice on both freeholders and leaseholders, so always put a healthy budget in for party walls and allow plenty of time.

Another thing to be aware of is Network Rail or other transport infrastructure. Aside from party walls, it has a legal contract called an Asset Protection Agreement (which can be basic or standard) which is designed to protect its infrastructure from any fallout from neighbouring building works. It is another hoop you have to jump through before you can build anything and unsurprisingly costs a lot of money and takes an age to do so. You may see lots of sites for sale that are bordering the railway, our advice is to tread very carefully!

SALES AND MARKETING

Sales and marketing costs	% sales	Cost (£)
Marketing (collateral & other)	0.25%	5,635
Agents fees	1.25%	28,174
Conveyancing costs on sales	0.5%	12,000
Total marketing costs		**45,809**

Please note, this table may not add up due to rounding.

Table A1.8 Sales and marketing costs

When thinking about collateral, you may want to produce some CGIs, a brochure or a website. Some developers pay up to 3% on marketing, but for a small, three-house scheme, a much more modest budget should suffice.

OTHER COSTS

Special Purpose Vehicle (SPV) costs		Cost (£)
SPV set-up fee (JV legals)		500
SPV managment costs	0%	0
Total SPV costs		**500**
Total Payments exc. finance		

Table A2.9 Other costs

Finance Costs	% of cost	Cost (£)	
Total debt	80%	1,396,455	
Total equity	20%	349,114	
Finance costs	% loan		
Arrangement fee	1.5%	19,969	
Exit fee	1.0%	13,313	
Broker fee	1.0%	13,313	
Legals	0.5%	6,656	
PM fee	0.5%	6,656	
Valuation	0.1%	1,331	
Total finance costs		**61,238**	
Interest rate	10.0%		
Planning (months)		12	
Tender (months)		6	36,855
Construction (months)		14	121,437

Table A2.10 Finance costs

Working down the list of other costs you should allow for a relatively small amount to set up the SPV. If you have investors or a complicated structure, this may cost more than in our simple example.

Arranging the debt doesn't come for free, so on top of the interest rate you have to pay fees so you should be budgeting for arrangement fees, exit fees, broker fees, valuation fees and legal fees.

It's worth thinking about when you draw down the debt. Your lender will normally give you the opportunity to draw it down in phases as you need it. Unless you are paying a commitment fee for undrawn money, you will only be paying interest at the point you draw the debt down. You will see that we don't apply an interest rate during the planning phase as banks will probably not lend you any money before a site has planning permission.

Now you have filled in all of the above, you should have a good idea of what your 'costs of everything else' will be and we can work out the profit of the development.

PROFIT

Total Costs inc. finance	1,883,592
Total Sales	2,253,912
Total Profit	**370,320**
Profit on costs	20%

Table A1.11 Profit calculation

In the example given, there is a healthy 20% profit on costs. If you are not happy with that number as a return, you need to play with all the assumptions. Perhaps you can sell your homes for more or build them for less. This is an iterative process and your adjustments will depend on your attitude to risk and how much you like the opportunity. You might decide to accept a lower profit on cost margin, when the housing market is rising and when you can assume market risk is lower and there is more certainty about estimated GDV. Or maybe the risk is lower because the site already has planning permission, so there is no need to take the risk on planning.

On the other hand, if the housing market is shaky, or build costs are going up, or the risk of planning is high, you may not want to accept a profit margin of less than 25%.

Don't forget that if you need to raise funding, it's not just yourself you have to convince, you also have to persuade investors and banks to lend you the money and neither like to do that on a project which has a margin of less than 15–20% unless there's a very good reason.

This is why the value of land can be more of an art than a science and only you can arrive at a figure that makes you comfortable.

APPENDIX B
SAMPLE LETTERS TO LANDOWNERS

Name
Address
Date

Dear [xxx]
Re: Your land at [site address]
I see that you are the owner of the above site. We are in the process of trying to find a site for our client and we think your site could be good for them.
I am contacting various landowners as we have the budget to buy a site and your site is on the list. Would you be interested in selling the land for £[xxx]? We would also pay all your (reasonable) legal costs.

Please let me know and I can issue you with a simple document to sign to get the legal process going straight away.

Thanks for your time.

Yours sincerely,

Name
Address
Date

Dear [xxx]
Re: Your land at [site address]
We hope you don't mind us getting in touch.
We are interested in land in the [xxx] area, and were wondering if we could have a discussion about the above site?
We specialise in design-led development, which is currently being promoted by the London Mayor, Government and the National Planning Policy Framework. We have identified your piece of land as a development opportunity and would like to know if you would consider selling.
What can we offer you?

- Speed – we will move quickly.
- Money – we have funds at our disposal to deploy on suitable sites.
- Experience – we are experienced property professionals and can design the best scheme on your site.

If any of the above is of interest, please telephone me on [xxx] or email me at [xxx].

Yours sincerely,

ENDNOTES

CHAPTER 1

1 Interview conducted between John Smart, Amanda Baillieu and Gus Zogolovitch, 27 April 2022.
2 Ibid.
3 Interview conducted between Jake Edgley, Amanda Baillieu and Gus Zogolovitch, 26 April 2022.
4 Jane Hall, 'We wanted to do things ourselves', in Harriet Harriss, Rory Hyde and Roberta Marcaccio (eds), *Architects After Architecture: Alternative Pathways for Practice* (Routledge, 2020), p. 137.
5 Gino Spoccia, 'Cost of living crisis: Can you still afford to be an architect in 2023?' *Architects Journal,* 13 December 2022, https://www.architectsjournal.co.uk/news/cost-of-living-crisis-can-you-still-afford-to-be-an-architect-in-2023 [accessed 30 March 2023].
6 Interview conducted between David Mikhail, Amanda Baillieu and Gus Zogolovitch, 8 March 2022.
7 Interview conducted between Dennis Hauer, Amanda Baillieu and Gus Zogolovitch, 8 March 2022.
8 Ibid.
9 Please note that the principles of development are the same throughout the world, but the book mainly refers to laws and common practices in England and Wales, so always seek local advice. Please also note that for the same reason, we don't generally talk about tax treatment as it varies so much geographically and over time. Instead, we would strongly advise you to seek specialist help.
10 Interview conducted between Sophie Goldhill, Amanda Baillieu and Gus Zogolovitch, 8 March 2022.
All subsequent quotes in this case study are from this interview.

CHAPTER 2

1 If Project A has an ROI of 30% and Project B has an ROI of 50% you might think that Project B is a better bet. However, if I then told you Project A is a year-long project and Project B will take 10 years, you'd know that Project A is the better bet. In this case, Project A would have an approximate IRR of 30% and Project B would have an approximate IRR of 4% which is a much easier way to compare the projects. Although note that this also doesn't tell the whole story. If I now said that Project A is investing in a start-up and Project B is putting the money in the bank, you may think again.
2 Throughout the book we will refer to land, but it is equally relevant if you buy a building and knock it down or buy a building and refurbish it or build on top of it.
3 For example, cost of construction, planning, professional fees, interest, etc.
4 Interview conducted between Catherine Burd, Amanda Baillieu and Gus Zogolovitch, 7 March 2022.
All subsequent quotes in this case study are from this interview.
5 Interview conducted between Diana Borland, Amanda Baillieu and Gus Zogolovitch, 15 July 2022.
All subsequent quotes in this case study are from this interview.
6 Crowdfunding is a form of raising money from multiple different investors and can be used to raise equity and/or debt. See chapter 5 for more information.

CHAPTER 3

1 Interview conducted between Carl Turner, Amanda Baillieu and Gus Zogolovitch, 27 April 2022.
2 Ibid.
3 https://www.jctltd.co.uk/ [accessed 22 March 2023].
4 Jack Airey, *Rethinking the Planning System for the 21st Century* (Policy Exchange, 2020), p.55.
5 Interview conducted between Richard Keys, Amanda Baillieu and Gus Zogolovitch, 26 April 2022.
6 Adverse possession is when someone who doesn't own some land acquires it because they've been using it for a very long time and the person who does actually own it has never told them to stop using it. It normally requires that person to have fenced off the land for at least 12 years. It's a tricky and difficult piece of very old legislation that you should always seek specialist advice on.
7 'Prior transfers' refer to all of the previous changes in ownership.
8 Interview conducted between Jeremy McLeod, Amanda Baillieu and Gus Zogolovitch, 26 April 2022.
All subsequent quotes in this case study are from this interview.

CHAPTER 4

1 Sophie Rosier and Tom Genner, 'London's housing crisis: Is public sector land the answer?', Savills Blog, https://www.savills.co.uk/blog/article/338067/residential-property/london-s-housing-crisis--is-public-sector-land-the-answer-.aspx [accessed 23 March 2023].
2 The 'Greater Fool' theory is the idea that, during a market bubble, you can make money by buying overvalued assets and selling them for a profit later on the basis that it will always be possible to find someone who is willing to pay a higher price.

3 Interview conducted between Donald Matheson, Amanda Baillieu and Gus Zogolovitch, 7 March 2022.
4 When searching for plots offered by local councils and public landowners, the 'Small Sites Small Builders' programme in London, run by the Greater London Authority on behalf of Transport for London (TfL), is a fruitful place to start. In its first round in 2017, TfL had 10 sites, all left-over bits of infill, which went for open market competition, attracting 180 bids.
5 Interview conducted between Maria Sjölander and Marco da Cruz, Amanda Baillieu and Gus Zogolovitch, 26 April 2022. All subsequent quotes in this case study are from this interview.
6 Conditional contract means that you buy once the condition has been met. Unconditional means a straightforward purchase. We explore these terms in more detail in chapter 6.
7 Interview conducted between John Smart, Amanda Baillieu and Gus Zogolovitch, 27 April 2022. All subsequent quotes in this case study are from this interview.
8 Interview conducted between David Mikhail, Amanda Baillieu and Gus Zogolovitch, 8 March 2022. All subsequent quotes in this case study are from this interview.

CHAPTER 5

1 Not all debt is the same. The higher up the pecking order you are, the less risk you take. Main lending institutions take first charge, which means they get paid first in the event of a liquidation. This is also known as 'senior debt'. Second charge, or 'junior debt', means that the lender gets paid second, which could result in not getting all their money back and is therefore more expensive (i.e. higher interest rates).
2 Typical interest rate (at time of writing) for a development finance loan.
3 It used to be linked to LIBOR – the London Interbank Offered Rate – but this is now being phased out due to various scandals and is being replaced by 'risk-free rates'.
4 See Appendix A for a more detailed look at the appraisal.
5 Take your rental income and divide it by the value of the property.
6 Note that these examples do not take into account tax (which is a whole book in itself) and are purely to show the relationship between equity and debt.
7 Interview conducted between Donald Matheson, Amanda Baillieu and Gus Zogolovitch, 7 March 2023. All subsequent quotes in this case study are from this interview.
8 'How to develop small sites' Conference run by Developer Collective, April 2018.

9 Interview conducted between Alex Wright, Amanda Baillieu and Gus Zogolovitch, 25 January 2023. All subsequent quotes in this case study are from this interview.

CHAPTER 6

1 In theory, if a seller doesn't sell the land on planning, you have recourse to sue for breach of contract and can sue for your costs and ultimately for the seller to have to sell you the land.
2 Planning is granted under permitted development rights. In theory it's supposed to be a simple process, although beware as 'on the ground' it's proving anything but. This subject is outside the scope of this book, but it is worth you increasing your understanding of planning so that you can properly brief your planning consultants.
3 Interview conducted between John Kinsley, Amanda Baillieu and Gus Zogolovitch, 15 July 2022. All subsequent quotes in this case study are from this interview.
4 Interview conducted between Jake Edgley, Amanda Baillieu and Gus Zogolovitch, 26 April 2022. All subsequent quotes in this case study are from this interview.
5 Interview conducted between George Ferguson, Amanda Baillieu and Gus Zogolovitch, 7 March 2022. All subsequent quotes in this case study are from this interview.
6 Ernest Hall transformed the derelict Dean Clough complex in Halifax, West Yorkshire, into a striking example of urban regeneration.

CHAPTER 7

1 Interview conducted between Carl Turner, Amanda Baillieu and Gus Zogolovitch, 27 April 2022.
2 Interview conducted between David Mikhail, Amanda Baillieu and Gus Zogolovitch, 8 March 2022.
3 Interview conducted between Mark Shaw, Amanda Baillieu and Gus Zogolovitch, 15 July 2022. All subsequent quotes in this case study are from this interview.
4 Interview conducted between Carl Turner, Amanda Baillieu and Gus Zogolovitch, 27 April 2022. All subsequent quotes in this case study are from this interview.

CHAPTER 8

1 Interview conducted between Maria Sjölander and Marco da Cruz, Amanda Baillieu and Gus Zogolovitch, 26 March 2022.
2 The Modern House started in 2005 and has been hugely influential in driving the desire for architecturally designed homes and making the Modernism movement desirable.
3 Interview conducted between Donald Matheson, Amanda Baillieu and Gus Zogolovitch, 7 March

2022.

4 It's not uncommon for purchases to be about 1% of the number of people who enter the 'top' of the funnel.

5 Interview conducted between Sophie Goldhill, Amanda Baillieu and Gus Zogolovitch, 8 March 2022.

6 As an example, if you have borrowed £2,000,000 at 8% per annum, then after 2 years, since you pay interest on the interest rolled up through the development, you will be paying approximately £4,000 per week in interest costs. A typical sale may take between 2 months to 4 months – which will cost you £35,000 to £70,000 interest costs alone.

7 Roger Fisher and William Ury, *Getting to Yes: Negotiating an Agreement without Giving In* (Cornerstone Digital, 2012) or Chris Voss and Tahl Raz, *Never Split the Difference: Negotiating as if Your Life Depended on It* (Random House, 2017).

8 Interview conducted between Oliver Thornton, Amanda Baillieu and Gus Zogolovitch, 26 April 2022. All subsequent quotes in this case study are from this interview.

9 Interview conducted between Cary Tamarkin, Amanda Baillieu and Gus Zogolovitch, 15 July 2022. All subsequent quotes in this case study are from this interview.

CHAPTER 9

1 Interview conducted between Cary Tamarkin, Amanda Baillieu and Gus Zogolovitch, 15 July 2022.

APENDIX A

1 A note about square foot and square meter. The property industry can't seem to make up its mind whether it is imperial or metric. 1m2 = 10.764 ft2. For some reason, sales seems to be in a price per square foot and building can often be in a price per square metre.

2 XXX means you should fill in your own data

3 Stamp duty is best calculated using an online stamp duty calculator.

4 Some local authorities have a set tax payable on net new development. London boroughs also have a Mayoral CIL charge. This is a complex area, so well worth seeking guidance from the Local Authority itself

INDEX

Note: page numbers in bold refer to tables.

IMAGE CREDITS

Figure 1.1, 1.2, 1.3, 1.4, 1.5 Liddicoat & Goldhill;

2.1, 2.2, 2.3, 2.4, 2.5, 2.6, 2.7 Burd Haward. Photography © Heather Hobhouse;

2.8, 2.9, 2.10 Harrison Hunt. Images courtesy www.paulmcmullin.com;

2.8, 2.9, 2.10 Harrison Hunt. Images courtesy © Paul McMullin (www.paulmcmullin.com);

3.1, 3.2 ByOthers;

3.3, 3.4, 3.5, 3.6, 3.7, 3.8, 3.9, 3.10 Breathe Architecture;

4.1, 4.2, 4.3, 4.4, 4.5, 4.6, 4.7, 4.8, 4.9, 4.10 Sjölander da Cruz Architects;

4.11, 4.12, 4.13, 4.14, 4.15 Craftworks. Photography: Edward Sumner;

4.16, 4.17, 4.18, 4.19 Mikhail Riches. Photography: Tim Crocker;

5.1, 5.2, 7.1, 8.1 RIBA Publishing;

5.3, 5.4, 5.5, 5.6, 5.7, 5.8 Matheson Whiteley. Photography: Maris Mazulis;

5.9, 5.10, 5.11, 5.12 Alex Wright;

6.1, 6.2, 6.3, 6.4, 6.5, 6.6, 6.7 John Kinsley Architects. Photography: John Reiach;

6.8, 6.9, 6.10, 6.11, 6.12 Edgley Design. Photography: Jack Hobhouse;

6.13, 6.14, 6.16 George Ferguson with Ferguson Mann;

6.15 George Ferguson with Ferguson Mann. Photography: Mark Dawson Photography;

7.2, 7.3, 7.4, 7.5, 7.6, 7.7, 7.8, 7.9 Studioshaw;

7.10, 7.11, 7.12, 7.13, 7.14 Turner Works. Photography: Tim Crocker;

7.15 Turner Works. Photography: Rory Gardiner;

8.2 Raw Property. Photography: Johan Eldrot;

8.3, 8.4 Raw Property. Photography: Sebastian Thorén;

8.5, 8.6 Raw Property. Photography: Martin Wichardt;

8.7, 8.8 Tamarkin Co./CT Architect. Photography: Bart Michiels;

8.9 Tamarkin Co./CT Architect;